London 2012
training guide

Athletics –
Track events

From beginner to champion

John Brewer

CARLTON

Contents

Foreword by Steve Cram MBE

I have had the great honour and privilege of competing at multiple Olympic Games, World Championships, European Championships and Commonwealth Games. In 1984, I stood on the podium after the Olympic Games 1,500 metres final, collecting a silver medal and, looking back, it was one of the greatest moments of my career.

Training for an event such as the Olympic Games required huge amounts of application, dedication, sacrifice and perseverance from me and those around me. It is important to acknowledge that I was supported by Team GB coaches and trainers, as well as my personal coaches, physiotherapists, family and friends, without whom my success would have been quite impossible.

This *London 2012 Training Guide* will help you on your way. Everyone knows how to run, but in these pages you will pick up techniques that will make you feel fitter, faster, more self-confident and able to reach competitive levels you thought were probably impossible.

It won't happen overnight, but if you dedicate yourself, you can achieve what most people consider impossible – Olympic glory.

Steve Cram, MBE

Introduction

Athletics is an iconic sport, epitomising the highest standards of human performance. Providing a range of opportunities for young and old, and sitting at the heart of the Olympic movement, it attracts recreational athletes from around the world who gain from the health and social benefits that the sport provides.

Our bodies are designed to run. In the distant past, our ancestors had to run to catch their food – or from predators looking for their own food! But unfortunately, modern societies have removed much of the need to exercise and run from our lives – cars, remote controls and computers now mean that for many people the hardest exercise they have is the walk from their car to the office or climbing the stairs to bed. Inevitably, illnesses linked to a lack of exercise – such as obesity and high cholesterol – are on the increase, and the health of many of the world's nations is on the decline.

But track athletics offers people of all ages a chance to reverse this trend and provides an opportunity for individuals to take part in sport and exercise on a regular basis. While for many the image of athletics is of lean and super-fit athletes taking part in the Olympic Games and World Championships, a thriving club structure, the development of the sport in schools and veterans events allow many people to train and compete from their school days until well into their later years. Even if not competing, the sport offers opportunities for a large cohort of volunteers and officials, including coaches, timekeepers and starters, all of whom gain from the social benefits that the association with athletics brings. While athletics is normally classified as an individual sport, the camaraderie and team spirit that are part of many clubs is no different to any other sports – clubs compete in leagues where the performances of each individual contribute to the final team score, and athletes frequently train together in groups, pushing and encouraging each other to better performances.

Today, there are opportunities for people of all standards to compete in track events, with clubs welcoming those who want to train, officiate or compete. A coaching structure provides support and encouragement for runners of all abilities, something that continues

The Olympic Games may be the ultimate achievement but athletes of all standards can compete in track athletics.

throughout the track season and the winter months, when runners move from the track to road and cross country events.

For many, the Olympic Games are seen as the pinnacle of track athletics, with the very best athletes from around the world taking part in events from the 100 metres to the 26.2 miles (42.2 kilometres) of the Marathon. The title of Olympic champion is one that all athletes aspire to at some point in their careers, but only a very few – with the right combination of training, physiology and coaching – ever attain that accolade. Nevertheless, the inspiration provided by the Olympic Games to many millions of people around the world encourages young and old to take part in track events, and gain the health and social benefits that one of the world's most popular and iconic sports can offer.

The basics

Track Athletics is one of the simplest and oldest of all sports at the Olympic Games, pitting individuals against each other in a quest to reach the finishing line as quickly as possible. This challenge places extreme demands on the human body, creating a spectacle that remains as compelling today as it was in the days of the Ancient Greeks.

Track events

Track events have a place at the heart of the Olympic movement and are at the forefront of each and every Olympic Games. However, track Athletics is much more than just an Olympic sport, providing individuals of all ages and abilities with the opportunity to train, compete, officiate and coach.

The Popularity of Athletics

Athletics is based on the core human movement of running, a natural human activity that can encompass anything from maximum-effort sprinting to slow, steady endurance running. Many individuals who compete on the track also do so in road running or in cross-country races, often during the winter months outside of the normal track season. Indeed, the recent growth in road running in the UK is testimony to the popularity of an activity that has spread far and wide. In the UK, for example, Sport England's third 'Active People' survey suggested that by 2009, 1.8 million people were taking part regularly in some form of athletics, while in the United States, the running population was estimated at a staggering 38.9 million in 2008, an increase of 18 per cent compared to the previous year.

These figures indicate that the sport has huge popularity, as well as large benefits for the health and wellbeing of the population. Many of the world's largest road races, such as the London and New York Marathons, frequently attract entry fields in excess of 35,000 runners, something that would have been unheard of just 30 years ago.

School and Club Athletics

In the UK, athletics is promoted from an early age in schools. There are many schemes that encourage children to take part in track athletics, including Sportshall athletics, which enables children to train and compete indoors during the winter, and United Kingdom athletics' grass roots programme, Startrack, which provides opportunities for coaching and training outside of school times. Young athletes can progress by representing their school at local and county events, with the very best selected to represent their county at the annual English Schools Championships.

The transition from school to club sport is all important, and is often a time when many people drop out of sport altogether. However, in the

Track athletics pushes human performance to its very limits through science, coaching and technology.

UK, joining an athletics club has never been easier and is greatly helped by UK Athletics' club search facility on their website uka.org.uk (see Finding a Club on page 26). Alongside the growth of social networking sites, there are even internet-only clubs that attract members from all over the country, substituting the clubhouse for a website yet still fostering competition and training.

The sport has developed considerably since its birth at the Ancient Olympic Games – today athletics encourages participation, but it is also a sport where the very highest stands of physical fitness can be observed, pushing the boundaries of human performance to their very limits at the cutting edge of science, physiology, coaching and technology.

Sprints and middle distance events

Track athletics is a sport that provides a variety of physical challenges, from the short, explosive sprint of the 100m, to the speed and agility of the Hurdles, and the sustained endurance of the 26.2-mile Marathon and the 50-kilometre Race Walk.

Sprints

Often considered to be the most high profile of all track events, the sprints consist of the 100 metres, 200m, 400m, 100m Hurdles (women), 110m Hurdles (men), 400m Hurdles and the 4x100m and 4x400m relays. With the exception of the last legs of the 4x400m relay, all sprint events are run in lanes, and normally at maximum, or close to maximum, speed. Unlike other track races, the sprint events start from a crouching sprint start position using starting blocks that enable sprinters to produce large horizontal forces and rapid acceleration, often reaching speeds of around 25 miles per hour (40 kilometres per hour) over the shortest 100m distance. To maximise stride length and stride rate, sprinters focus on the development of both power and technique. Many sprinters also work to develop the strength and power of their upper bodies, to counter the rotational forces produced when accelerating and running at high speeds.

The middle distance events combine speed and distance as well as race tactics.

Middle Distance

The middle distance events are classified as the 800m, 1,500m and 3,000m Steeplechase. Middle distance athletes must have a unique combination of speed and endurance, which places heavy demands on their energy systems. With the exception of the first bend of elite 800m races, the middle distance events are not run in lanes. They tend to

The 100m and 200m sprints are breathtaking to watch as they are run at maximum speed.

be the most physical of all track events, with bumping and pushing a frequent occurrence in many races. It is rare to find a top middle distance runner who does not have good basic speed – the Kenyan athlete Wilson Kipketer's 800m world record of 1min 41.11secs, set in 1997, is equivalent to a time of 12.6secs for each 100m, while Moroccan Hicham El Guerrouj's 1,500m world record of 3:26.00 is only slightly slower, at 13.7secs per 100m.

The 3,000m Steeplechase places additional technical and physical demands on athletes, since it includes 28 barriers and seven water jumps. The race was added to the women's programme for the first time at the Beijing 2008 Olympic Games.

Long distance and Race Walking

Few other sports have the global recognition of track athletics, a reflection of the simplicity and history of the sport. Whether in an Olympic arena, or on a grass track in a field, the sport can be, and is, enjoyed by millions throughout the world.

Long Distance

The long distance – or endurance – events consist of the 5,000 metres, 10,000m and the 26.2 miles (42km) of the Marathon. These events are not run in lanes, and in Olympic competition the Marathon usually only starts and finishes in the stadium, with the majority of the race run on surrounding roads. The long distance events place a heavy aerobic demand on athletes, who need to transport large volumes of oxygen to their muscles to produce energy without causing fatigue. Because carrying excess weight increases the energy demands on the body, most long distance runners have lean physiques, with low body fat percentages and far less muscle mass than sprinters.

The speed that endurance runners must sustain should not be underestimated. It was only in 1954 that Sir Roger Bannister first broke the four-minute barrier for the mile, yet the current men's Marathon world record of 2hrs 3mins 59secs, held by Ethiopian Haile Gebrselassie, averages 4mins 43secs for each of the 26 miles, while the world record of 2:15.25, held by the UK's Paula Radcliffe, equates to 5mins and 10secs for each mile.

Long distance events place heavy aerobic demands on athletes.

Race Walking

Race Walking has its history in the
long distance 'pedestrianism' events
that were popular in England in the
19th century. In the Olympic Games,
both male and female walkers
compete over 20 kilometres and
50km distances, the latter being the
longest of all the track events held
at the Olympic Games.

It is governed by two rules: the
first is that the toe of the rear foot
cannot leave the ground until
the heel of the front foot has
touched the ground – in other
words there must be contact
at all times, and breaking
this rule is known as 'loss
of contact'; the second rule
states that the supporting leg
must remain straight until the
body has passed directly over it.
Judges continuously monitor these
rules during races and can disqualify
an athlete after three rule violations.

Race walkers tend to adopt a short
stride length and rapid cadence, a
style which is deemed most suitable to
remaining within the rules. Elite walkers
can achieve high speeds – the world
20km record of 1:16.43, held by
Russian Sergey Morozov, represents a
speed of close to 10 miles per hour
(16km per hour).

*Race walkers compete over long distances
but can still reach impressive speeds.*

Combined events

Since the birth of the Olympic Games, multi-event competitions have been held to find the most talented all-round athletes. Featuring a mix of both track and field events, and often held over two days, they test an athlete's fitness and technique to the limit in a quest to find the supreme all round champion.

For athletes who want to test their skills and prowess over a range of events, the Heptathlon (women) and Decathlon (men) provide an additional challenge. Multi-event athletes tend to develop great camaraderie during their two-day event, with the winners generally recognised as the best all-round athlete in the competition.

Track and Field
Of the seven events in the Heptathlon, only three are track events – the 100 metres hurdles, the 200m and the 800m. The remaining four are field events (High Jump, Shot Put, Javelin Throw and Long Jump), so athletes who excel at the Heptathlon tend to be those adept at anaerobic and power-based events, rather than those with high levels of aerobic endurance.

Similarly, of the ten events of the men's Decathlon only four are track events (100m, 110m hurdles, 400m and 1,500m) compared with six field events (Long Jump, High Jump, Shot Put, Pole Vault, Discus Throw and Javelin Throw), so also tend to favour the more explosive, anaerobic athlete.

The Competition
Both the Heptathlon and Decathlon are based on one of the most ancient of all Olympic events, the Pentathlon, when five events were held over a single day. In the current modern Olympic Games, the Heptathlon and Decathlon are held over two consecutive days and points are scored based on the standard of performance in each individual event. At the end of the two days of competition, the points for each event are totalled to find the overall winner. The points score for each event is based on a series of tables adopted by the IAAF in 1984, which try to ensure that the scores for similar standards of performance in each event are comparable.

Adopting a proper recovery strategy between each event is vital, with athletes continually having to warm up and warm down and prepare psychologically for their next event. Ensuring that hydration and energy intake are sustained without adversely impacting on performance is a further challenge, and as a result, gaining experience in multi-event competitions is an invaluable part of an athlete's development.

Training
If you are training for the Heptathlon or Decathlon, you will face a rigorous regimen of hard work to continually develop each aspect of your performance. The main focus of

your training will be the development of strength, power, technique and speed endurance, with only a relatively small amount of endurance running. It is rare to find specialist middle or long distance runners excelling at the Heptathlon or Decathlon, due to the nature of the other events that are part of the competition. Since the 800m (Heptathlon) and 1,500m (Decathlon) are the final events, most multi-event athletes will already be fatigued by the time these events commence, making it hard for specialists to perform well.

To triumph in either the Decathlon or Heptathlon is regarded as one of the pinnacles of Athletes.

The science of running

The human body has been designed to run, and has an incredible ability to respond and adapt to the stimulus of training. Understanding the scientific basis of exercise is the key to unlocking the body's physical and mental potential, and fundamental to the design of a training programme.

Running, like all forms of transport, requires energy. The human body gets its energy from the food and fluid that it consumes and stores it in two main forms – carbohydrate and fat – both of which can then be utilised to provide the energy needed to power the contraction and relaxation of muscles, as well as the function of critical organs such as the brain, kidneys and liver.

Stored Energy

While most humans have enough energy stored in their bodies to fuel around 40 consecutive Marathons, they normally only have enough carbohydrate stores for around two hours of moderate-intensity exercise. This would suggest – wrongly – that fat is an ideal fuel for track events. Unfortunately, fat is only capable of providing the body with energy at a slow rate, something that it does in combination with oxygen that is contained in air that is breathed in. Even in long distance events such as the Marathon and 10,000 metres, the rate of energy supply from fat is not normally rapid enough to meet the needs of most runners, so instead the body relies on its other fuel reserve, carbohydrate.

Aerobic Energy

Carbohydrates are stored in muscle and the liver as a substance called glycogen, which can provide energy at a more

The cardio-vascular system – showing the transport of oxygen and blood around the body

The heart – showing the four chambers that pump blood through the arteries and veins

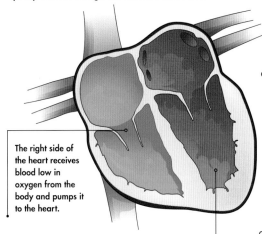

The right side of the heart receives blood low in oxygen from the body and pumps it to the heart.

The left side of the heart receives blood high in oxygen from the lungs and pumps it around the body.

events, the rate at which even the most efficient aerobic system enables carbohydrate and oxygen to provide energy is still not rapid enough to meet most athletes' energy needs. In these events, carbohydrate will still be the main source of energy, but this occurs without oxygen being present, using what is known as the body's anaerobic energy system. While the anaerobic system can provide energy very rapidly, the main drawback is that it produces by-products such as a substance called lactic acid, which quickly causes the body to fatigue. Of course, if it wasn't for this, the fastest sprinters would also be the quickest Marathon runners, and it is the role and interaction of both the aerobic and anaerobic energy systems that dictates the nature of training programmes that are specific to each track event.

rapid rate than fat. When glycogen (and fat) are converted to energy in conjunction with oxygen, the body uses what is known as its aerobic energy system. The aerobic system can provide a steady supply of energy with minimal fatigue. But one of the factors limiting the efficiency of the aerobic system is known to be the rate at which oxygen can be supplied to the muscles, and as we will see later in this book, one of the main aims of any training programme is to enhance the efficiency of the aerobic system and increase the rate at which oxygen can be supplied to the muscles.

Anaerobic Energy
However, in sprint events, and indeed many of the middle distance

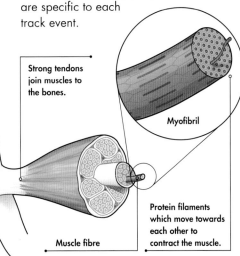

Strong tendons join muscles to the bones.

Myofibril

Protein filaments which move towards each other to contract the muscle.

Muscle fibre

A brief history

Records of athletes competing against each other exist since ancient times, but in recent years the desire to push the boundaries of physical performance has increased. Track athletics attracts global audiences, and many of the sport's stars have global recognition and fame.

Olympic Origins

Track athletics has its roots in early history, with the first ever recorded race being the 'stadion footrace' held at the first Ancient Olympic Games in Greece in 776 BC.

The classic 'stadion' distance for the oval running track of 192 metres became the standard distance for track events for many years and later became the basis from which the word 'stadium' was derived. The Games were held every four years in honour of Zeus, king of the Greek gods, and were named after the gods' home, Mount Olympus. The ancient Olympic Games evolved into a festival that included music and arts, but as the influence of the Romans and Christianity increased, the Games were banned in AD 393.

Athletics in Europe

During this period track athletics spread into Europe, reaching Italy in around 200 BC. More events were added as the sport grew alongside field and multi-event competitions such as the Javelin Throw, Discus Throw and Pentathlon. Until the 1800s, track events were always held as part of general sporting festivals, but at around this time the sport began to appear as distinct competitions, often with handicapping and betting as an integral part of races. The Steeplechase and Hurdles events were introduced in England in the mid-1800s, born out of the cross country and 'harrier' races that had gained large popularity by this time, and in 1880 the first national governing body for the sport in England – the Amateur

Jesse Owens

Jesse Owens was a black American athlete, born in Alabama in 1913. He suffered racial discrimination for most of his career, before competing in the Berlin 1936 Olympic Games. He won four gold medals – in the 100m, 200m, 4x100m Relay and Long Jump – a remarkable feat equalled by fellow American Carl Lewis at the Los Angeles 1984 Games. At the victory ceremonies, Owens was notoriously snubbed by Adolf Hitler, who refused to shake his hand. After the Games, Owens unsuccessfully tried to earn money from professional sport, and shortly before his death in 1980 failed to persuade US President Jimmy Carter not to boycott the Moscow 1980 Olympic Games.

Track events were at the centre of the first Modern Olympic Games in Athens 1896.

Athletics Association – was established. The USA and France quickly followed suit, establishing their own governing bodies for athletics at the end of the same decade.

The Modern Olympic Games

After visiting the Much Wenlock Games, held in Shropshire, UK, for the first time in 1850, Frenchman Baron Pierre de Coubertin was inspired to create the Modern Olympic Games, and the first version of what has now become the largest sporting tournament on Earth was held in Athens in 1896. Athletics was one of the highlights of the early Olympic Games, and over the next few years more and more track events were added to the programme. Women's events were only introduced into the Olympic Games for the first time in 1928, and today, with the exception of the 100m Hurdles and 110m Hurdles, women compete over the same track distances as men.

Recent History

In 1912, the International Amateur Athletic Federation (IAAF) was formed, and remains today as the world governing body for the sport, currently having over 200 member nations. Throughout the 1960s, the sport increased in popularity, with more media exposure, which resulted in increased global popularity of athletes, all of whom remained true to the amateur ethos that was at the time an inherent part of the sport. But inevitably, top athletes began to realise that they had commercial value, and during the 1970s and 1980s there was increasing pressure to bow to professionalism in the sport. In 1983 the IAAF introduced its own World Athletics Championships. This event, like the Olympic Games, is held on a four-yearly cycle. Having abandoned the traditional concept of amateurism in 1982, the IAAF Congress agreed to re-brand the organisation as the International Association of Athletics Federations in 2001.

The growth of professionalism

During the 1980s, sports media coverage continued to grow, with individuals such as Sebastian Coe, Steve Ovett, Carl Lewis and Daley Thompson becoming celebrities as well as athletes.

Prize Money

Inevitably, the pressure to completely drop the amateur ethos that had been an inherent part of the sport since its inception increased still further. In the 1990s, the IAAF bowed to pressures to allow open professionalism in the sport, and in 1997 prize money was introduced at the World Championships for the first time. In 1998 the IAAF established the Golden League series of track and field competitions in Europe, with extensive prize money for competitors and winners attracting the very best athletes in the world. The series was replaced in 2010 by the IAAF Diamond League, with greatly increased financial rewards, and meetings in North America, the Middle East and Asia, as well as Europe.

The Inspiration of the Olympic Games

The current popularity of track athletics owes much to its status as a flagship sport within both the Ancient and Modern Olympic Games. In 2008, the Beijing Olympic Games attracted a global audience of 4.7 billion viewers – or around 70% of the

Michael Johnson

Born in Texas in 1967, Johnson is widely acknowledged as the greatest 400m runner of all time. Between 1993 and 1999 he won the 400m world title on four occasions, as well as winning the 200m world title twice. During his career he set world records in the 200m and 400m, and his 400m world record of 43.18secs, set in 1999, still stands. His first Olympic medal was gold as part of the US 4x400m Relay team at the Barcelona 1992 Olympic Games, and he won the 200m and 400m titles at the Atlanta 1996 Games. At Sydney 2000, he again won gold in the 400m, but injury prevented him from defending his 200m title. Although part of the winning USA 4x400m Relay team, he voluntarily returned his medal when team-mate Antonio Pettigrew was banned for using performance-enhancing drugs.

world's population – projecting Athletics and the other Olympic sports into millions of homes around the world. The Olympic motto "Citius, Altius, Fortius" (Faster, Higher, Stronger) is exemplified by Athletics, and the combination of speed, endurance, tactics and strength create a spectacle that captures the spirit and ethos of the Olympic Games. For the vast majority of athletes the Olympic Games remains the true pinnacle of the sport. Around the world, millions are inspired by watching the world's best track athletes compete in Olympic competition, and the title of Olympic champion is the one that the majority of athletes covet most.

Track athletics enjoys a high profile with its top athletes becoming international stars.

The athletics arena

A simple oval arena is the focal point of track athletics. Whether a high-tech all weather surface designed by scientists, or a simple grass track, it provides the opportunity for athletes to compete against each other in an environment that is both fair and accurate.

The Track

Evolving from the original 192-metre 'stadion' of the ancient Olympic Games, today's 400m athletics track consists of two parallel straights, linked together by two semicircular bends. The 400m distance is calculated from a point 30 centimetres in from the inside edge, and tracks are usually divided into between six and ten separate lanes. A lane must be between 122cm and 125cm in width, and these are numbered from 1 on the inside to higher numbers on the outside.

Lanes

In events from 100m to 400m, races are run throughout in lanes. In high-level 800m races, the first bend only is run in lanes. Any athlete touching the line separating the lanes with a foot is liable to be disqualified.

For the 200m and 400m events (including the Relay), and when appropriate the first bend of 800m races, all of which involve running around one or both of the bends, athletes in the outer lanes start ahead of those in the inner lanes. This is commonly known as the 'stagger', and is used to counteract the greater distance that is encountered when running around the outside of a bend, so that all athletes run the same distance.

Start and Finish Lines

In races of 1,500m and above, races are not run in lanes and athletes always start from a curved start line at the relevant point on the track. Whatever form of start line is used, the feet (or hands in the case of a sprint start) must remain behind the start line.

The 'home straight' is the straight along which the 100m and shorter Hurdle events are held. Regardless of the race distance, the finish line is always at the end of the home straight. The opposite straight is often referred to as the 'back straight'.

Timing Races

Races commence upon the firing of a gun by the starter, who is assisted by judges who ensure that all athletes are correctly

All track events are electronically timed and shown to spectators on scoreboards.

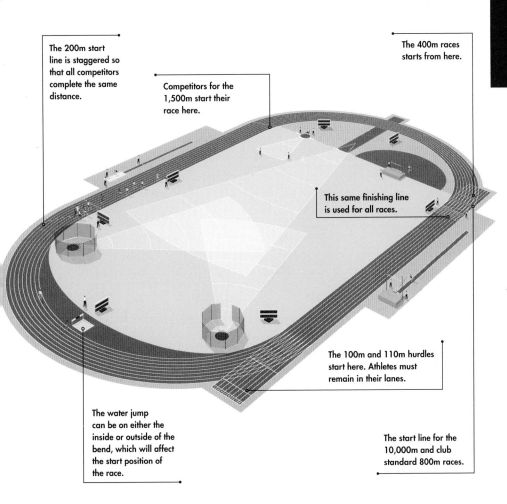

The 200m start line is staggered so that all competitors complete the same distance.

Competitors for the 1,500m start their race here.

The 400m races starts from here.

This same finishing line is used for all races.

The 100m and 110m hurdles start here. Athletes must remain in their lanes.

The water jump can be on either the inside or outside of the bend, which will affect the start position of the race.

The start line for the 10,000m and club standard 800m races.

positioned at the start. At the highest level, races will be timed electronically, beginning when the starter's gun fires and ceasing when athletes break an electronic beam with their upper torsos at the finish line. However, at most levels, including club athletics, events will be hand timed by judges based on a podium at the finish line, who will also determine finishing positions. When races are electronically timed, the need for judges to assess finishing positions is not required, and in the event of a close finish, a digital image, triggered when the finish line is breached, can provide a 'photo finish' to separate the athletes.

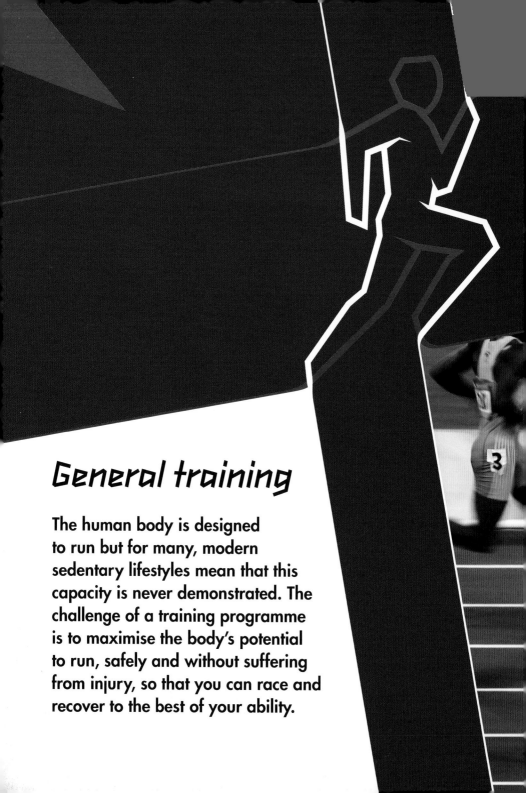

General training

The human body is designed to run but for many, modern sedentary lifestyles mean that this capacity is never demonstrated. The challenge of a training programme is to maximise the body's potential to run, safely and without suffering from injury, so that you can race and recover to the best of your ability.

Getting started

Getting the foundations in place for a successful running career is vital, whatever the ability of the athlete, and the distance they are considering running. Following simple guidelines, and gaining a basic knowledge of the principles of training, is crucial from the outset.

It is often said that if you want to become an Olympic champion, you need to select your parents carefully! However, regardless of genes, the human body can respond and adapt to the challenge presented by training, and while not everyone is capable of breaking world records, with correct and structured training, significant improvements in performance are possible.

Join Up!

If you are considering joining a club so that you can train and compete, it is important to find one that suits your needs. With some basic research you should be able to find the answers to these simple questions – What age group does it cater for? Does it compete on the track or on the road and cross country? When does it train and what coaching does it offer? Many clubs will welcome visits from prospective members (see box), allowing you to speak to members and see for yourself what facilities are on offer.

Training

There are five basic principles that any training programme must adhere to. These are:

Progression – A training programme must be progressive and gradually increase the workload that you are exposed to. Simply doing the same session over and over again will not lead to improvements.

Overload – Training must place a physiological 'overload' onto the body that is high enough to stimulate changes, yet not so high that it causes fatigue or injury. Combining the first two principles of training, by progressively overloading the body, is one of the keys to a successful training programme. This can be achieved by

Finding a Club

United Kingdom Athletics (UKA), the national governing body for the sport in the UK, provide a club search facility on their website uka.org.uk Use this to find a club near to your home and then pay a visit to check out the facilities and coaching. Speak with existing members to see if the club offers the type of training and competitive environment that suits your needs, and what age groups it best caters for. See if the club will let you go along a couple of times to take part in training sessions before making up your mind about joining.

Finding a club and structured training by a qualified coach are the foundations of a rewarding athletics career.

following the 'FITT' principle, changing some or all of the following factors:

- Frequency of training
- Intensity of training
- Time (duration) of training
- Type of training

Specificity – Training must be specific to your event and, of course, must be based on running. While there is scope for variability and change, the bulk of the training must be closely linked to your event.

Recovery – Including sufficient recovery time in a training programme is essential, since it gives the body a chance to adapt to the stimulus created by training, and time to recover from injury and fatigue.

Reversibility – Unfortunately, the gains achieved from training will also be lost through inactivity. Therefore one of the key challenges is to include sufficient recovery time, without risking the loss of any training gains.

Training safety

For anyone who hasn't exercised for some time, the demands of a training programme may be a shock to the body's systems. A few simple checks, and perhaps a visit to a GP, should help to ensure that everything is in shape to benefit from a sensible introduction to exercise and training.

Since one of the main principles of training is to place an overload on the body in excess of that found during normal daily activities, it is essential that if you plan to start a training programme you first undertake some basic health checks.

Athletics is a sport that anyone can start, at any age, so having a health check is even more important if you are older, or if it has been some time since you last took part in physical exercise. Here are some simple tests that you can do:

BMI

This test assesses your weight by checking your Body Mass Index (or BMI). It is calculated by dividing body weight (in kilograms) by height (in metres) squared. For example, an individual weighing 75kg and 1m 70 centimetres tall would have a BMI of 75 divided by (1.7 x 1.7), or 75 divided by 2.9 = 25.9 (overweight category – see box).

BMI scores	
Underweight	< 18.5
Normal weight	18.5–24.9
Overweight	25–29.9
Obese	> 30

Waist Circumference

Some doctors claim that waist circumference is a better indicator of heart and cardiovascular disease than BMI. Waist circumferences in excess of 80cm and 94cm for women and men respectively indicate risk, while those measuring above 88cm for women and 102cm for men are of particular concern.

How to find a coach

In the UK, the best coaches will have qualified through the UK Athletics Coach Education Programme. This programme trains coaches in the basic principles of coaching, while also enabling them to specialise in specific disciplines or events. There are four levels to the UKA Coach Education Programme, with Level 4 being the highest and taking at least 18 months to complete. Additionally, there are two Leaders Awards that focus on Children in Athletics, and Fitness in Running and Walking. When you visit a club, check out the qualifications of the coaches to ensure you get the right level of support and advice for your needs.

Waist–Hip Ratio

The 'waist–hip ratio' is the ratio of waist circumference (the narrowest point on the abdomen) to hip circumference (the widest point on the abdomen). If the waist–hip ratio is found to exceed 1 for a man (the waist is bigger than the hips), or 0.8 for a woman, this suggests an urgent need to lose weight and do more exercise.

Medical Check-up

Of course, these relatively simple measures will not reveal any underlying medical conditions that you might have – if you have any concerns about your health it is advisable to see your doctor for a more comprehensive check-up – which might include measures of heart and lung function, blood pressure and cholesterol, as well as more general advice on lifestyle, eating and drinking habits – before embarking on a physical exercise programme.

Role of a Coach

A good coach will know how to safely structure and develop a training programme in a manner that meets your needs and capabilities so that you gain the maximum benefits without risking injury. For these reasons, it is worth training with a coach.

Athletics puts a lot of demands on your body so you should undertake some health checks before you begin.

Overtraining

Doing too much too soon can easily be a problem, especially when the motivation to train is high, and the rapid gains that occur at the start of a training programme are easily apparent. Understanding when to rest is crucial as it is a fundamental part of an athlete's training programme.

Training Levels

All successful athletes need to be able to push themselves, often to the brink of injury. As you seek to improve your performances, you will have to train harder because as you approach your genetic limits, there are inevitably diminishing returns from each increase in training volume and intensity. The key to success is to understand how hard to push, and how much recovery to include in a training programme to give your body a chance to rest and adapt to the training stimulus.

Unfortunately, in the desire to improve, many athletes fail to include sufficient recovery in their training and often experience either a rapid decline in performance or injury. This is often referred to as 'overtraining', and can occur to both experienced and novice athletes alike. It is worth remembering that a training programme that can easily be accomplished by an experienced athlete may be too hard for a beginner, and you are often at the greatest risk of overtraining simply because you may increase the intensity of your training too quickly.

Fatigue

If you are a part-time athlete, combining training with a busy work and personal life, it can be the cumulative effect of your lifestyle, and not just the training alone, that leads to overtraining and fatigue. Of course, almost all athletes will experience some fatigue as a result of their training and this is perfectly normal. The skill is to recognise the abnormal symptoms of chronic fatigue, such as poor sleep patterns, irritability and frequent illnesses and injuries, and do everything possible to prevent these occurring or getting worse. Prevention is normally more than just rest – it involves recognising that training and lifestyles are becoming too intense or too addictive, and making a conscious effort to change.

Prevention

It is generally accepted that endurance athletes are the most likely to overtrain, simply because of the high distances that are covered in training. Fortunately, since overtraining tends to be a gradual, rather than a sudden process, it is

Professional athletes appreciate that rest and recovery are crucial elements of a training scheme.

possible to recognise the symptoms and prevent the problem from getting worse. Complete rest is often not necessary, and with a coach you can work to include more rest into a programme and reduce the volume and intensity of the training programme.

For beginners without a coach, avoiding the temptation to do 'too much too soon' is imperative, especially when starting out on a training regimen. Simply listening to your body and being prepared to take time off to rest or recover is crucial. While it may seem as if a few days off will lead to a decline in fitness, in the long term it is much better to take this step than to continue overtraining and allow more serious problems to develop.

Training clothing and equipment

Track athletics requires little in the way of expensive kit. But in the quest for improved knowledge, understanding and performance, science and technology have combined to provide athletes with a choice of equipment that could make the difference between winning and losing.

Clothing

Compared with many sports, the clothing required for track events is relatively simple. The normal apparel for competition consists of a running vest and shorts. Regulations state that this must be non-transparent (including when wet) and not likely to cause offence. If you are competing for a club, you will be required to wear the club colours, as well as identification numbers. Numbers are also worn on the shorts and side of the leg to help with identification in events where photo-finish technology is available.

When training away from a track or in a non-competitive environment, wear clothing that is appropriate for the conditions, such as T-shirts and wet tops. It is essential that clothing is comfortable and not likely to produce abrasions or blisters. The risk of abrasions can be reduced through the application of petroleum jelly to potentially susceptible areas such as the feet and inner thighs.

Shoes

Running shoes are often referred to as running spikes, after the metal spikes that are screwed into the base. Up to 11 spikes are permitted in each shoe, with a maximum length of 9 millimetres on synthetic surfaces and 11mm on non-synthetic surfaces. The maximum diameter of each spike is 4mm.

When training on roads or trails, you are more likely to wear training shoes and not spikes, which provide support and cushioning to reduce the risk of injury. There are many styles of training shoe available at a range of prices, many of which are designed to accommodate a particular running style. Visit a reputable running shop where advice from staff should be available to help you identify the most appropriate running shoe for your needs.

Heart Rate Monitors

Advances in technology have brought about the introduction of various aids to help with training, most of which are of greatest benefit to middle distance and endurance runners. The most popular of these are heart rate monitors, consisting of a device similar in shape and size to a wristwatch and a lightweight chest strap. These can be used to give a real time reading of your heart rate level or can store data that can be downloaded afterwards to provide a record of heart rate levels for the duration of a training session. Heart rate monitors can be used to provide an indication of training intensity, helping to reduce the risk of overtraining.

Other devices used by runners include Global Positioning Systems, which enable the distance covered during a training session to be accurately monitored. There are also an increasing number of websites that enable you to find running routes near to your home or to plot and measure the distance you have covered while training.

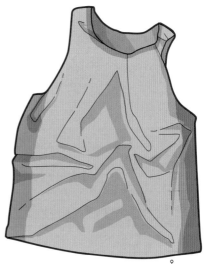

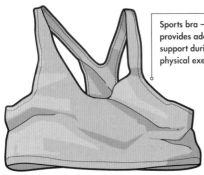

Sports bra – provides additional support during physical exercise.

A training vest – worn over another item of clothing on cold days.

Heart rate monitors can provide an indication of training intensity, helping to reduce the risk of overtraining.

Running shoes – take advice from a specialist shop about which model is best for you.

Training shorts – these offer freedom of movement, but some athletes prefer Lycra shorts.

What do you want to achieve?

Whilst many athletes aspire to become an Olympic champion, for many others the desire to train and compete is more closely linked with goals such as improved fitness or loss of weight. Setting targets not only provides motivation, but is also a means of assessing progress.

Motivation

There are many reasons why people participate in sport, with a corresponding range of desired outcomes. For some highly talented athletes, there is a genuine desire to succeed on the international stage and to win major championships. For others, it may be the companionship that being part of a club and a sport can bring, or the desire to compete regularly and just do as well as possible. Specific problems may provide some with the motivation to train – the need to lose weight is often one of the most common drivers behind sports participation.

Setting Targets

In setting targets, it is important to consider your short-, medium- and long-term goals, all of which should be both realistic and attainable. If you are a beginner, simply completing a training run without having to stop might be a short-term target, while achieving a personal best over one or more race distances might be a long-term target once you have been training for some time.

Most athletes will work with a coach on a regular basis to set, and then reset, realistic targets for their training and competing. There is a tendency for elite athletes to have more focused goals – such as the winning of a specific championship – than non-elite athletes, who often focus more on taking part and doing as well as possible.

For veteran athletes, continually trying

Your initial motivation may be to simply lose weight or get fitter but as your performances improve your targets can become more focused.

to set personal-best times becomes increasingly difficult with age, so setting an age-related target or trying to beat a time set within the last 12–24 months, might be more realistic and achievable.

By understanding what you want to achieve from your training and competing, it is possible for you and your coach to work together to devise programmes and strategies that can achieve your goals. This in itself provides positive feedback and encouragement, which in turn motivates you to set new targets.

Training plan

Incorporating regular training into your daily lifestyle is crucial for success in track athletics, so finding ways of making training habitual will help ensure that your training programme is successful and overcome the times when the motivation to train is low.

Sticking to the Plan

The actual training programme is often the easy bit, and can be designed in conjunction with a coach to ensure you work towards your goals safely and progressively. The real challenge is consistent adherence to the plan and this requires dedication, hard work and the support of family members. Alongside, it is also important that you develop an ability to understand your own body, responding to signs and signals so that training intensity and volume, and lifestyle, can be adjusted accordingly.

Weekly Plan

At the start of each week, you should know exactly what training has to be carried out over the coming seven days and plan your lifestyle around this. The successful completion of each training session should become the short-term daily target, with the completion of all of the sessions for the week the longer-term goal.

Training Log

Many athletes get into the habit of recording their training in a personal diary or training log, recording not only their training, but also other relevant aspects of their daily lives such as diet, how they feel, sleep patterns, recovery and how they felt after the training session.

A training log can become a useful guide for monitoring training progress, as well as acting as a motivational tool. It also serves as a reference tool so that you can reflect back and see what worked

---

A sample training log

Monday
Sleep: 8 hours
Pulse: 55
Weight: 67.5kg

Training: am 5 miles steady run, 30mins. Felt good.
pm Light weights session in gym, bit sore left hamstring.

Tuesday
Sleep: 8 hours
Pulse: 54
Weight: 67.3kg

Training: pm Track session, 6 x 400m, 1min recovery between 400s, target 63secs. 5mins jog, then repeat. Tired afterwards but hamstring OK.

Wednesday
Sleep: 8.5 hours
Pulse: 56
Weight: 67.3kg

Training: Rest day.

well and what worked badly. In this way you can gain a better understanding of the type of training and lifestyle that works best for you, and, equally importantly, understand what to avoid so that your performances are not undermined.

While all top athletes have their own coaches, with experience they start to understand what type of training and lifestyle best suits their individual needs, often using the coach as a mentor and guide, rather than someone who dictates every training session that they undertake.

Health and Wellbeing

There are some simple measures that you can take to monitor your general health and wellbeing. These include pulse rate, which is best taken on waking in the morning, as well as the number of hours of sleep and early morning body weight. Any large changes in either or all of these may be an indication of overtraining or illness and you should act sensibly by either reducing training or, if the symptoms persist, seek medical advice.

Careful planning, dedication and the support of family and friends are crucial.

Family Support

The nature of your lifestyle, which, among other things, will demand regular training and specific dietary requirements, inevitably means that your family has to become part of the support team. Family members will need to help you with travel, cooking, kit washing and morale support and encouragement, especially during tough training periods or if things aren't going well.

Intensity levels

Middle distance and endurance runners, whose events require a combination of aerobic and anaerobic energy, need to ensure that their training sessions provide the specific exercise intensity levels required to enhance performance.

The Right Level

In the past, some less informed coaches have applied the adage of 'no pain, no gain' when working with athletes, thus intimating that unless a training session was of maximum effort, and resulted in fatigue, there was little chance of it being of any benefit. In fact, scientific evidence has shown that continually trying to train at a high intensity quickly causes both physiological and psychological fatigue, not improved performance. While there is both scope and a need for high-intensity sessions, these must form only a part of a training programme. Conversely, if training is too easy, it is unlikely to produce a meaningful training effect. Therefore you need to establish a mix of low-, medium- and high-intensity training that produces optimum improvements in performance, allows scope for recovery and does not result in overtraining and chronic fatigue.

Heart Rate Monitors

One technique that can help is the use of heart rate monitors. There are many recommendations on the exact heart rate zones, but in general it is accepted that at an exercise heart rate below around 60–70 per cent of maximum there will be minimal training effect. The aerobic

energy system is best developed at an intensity of between 70 and 80 per cent of maximum heart rate. High-intensity training, developing a combination of the aerobic and anaerobic systems, occurs at between 80 and 90 per cent of maximum heart rate, while short-term near maximum-

effort work occurs at heart rates in excess of 90 per cent of maximum.

It is important to be aware that heart rate tends to creep up gradually with time, so it is best to start a session at the lower end of the range. Maximum heart rate also decreases with age (normally estimated by subtracting age from 220) and this needs to be factored in when converting a heart rate value to a percentage of maximum.

Finally, heart rate monitors are only a guide to training intensity and many athletes exercise perfectly well without them, often by getting a feel for the different intensity levels and the body's reaction to a training session.

Finding the right level of intensity in training is crucial. Too much exercise will fatigue you and too little will not improve your performances.

Basic training

For athletes involved in middle distance and long distance events, a solid endurance base needs to be developed before training can progress. For sprinters, some endurance is important to support further training, but the main foundations come in the form of core stability and strength.

Running

Developing an endurance base to support training and competition is essential and inevitably requires hard work and determination. Due to the specificity of training, the vast majority of work to develop endurance comes from running, which develops the cardiovascular system to ensure an efficient supply of blood and oxygen to the muscles, as well as strengthening and developing the aerobic capacity of the muscles, particularly those in the legs where much of the energy-producing work is undertaken. While non-running activities such as cycling and swimming will have an effect on the cardiovascular system, the demands will not be the same as those encountered when running, nor will there be the localised yet crucial developments within the muscles of the legs.

A Gradual Build-up

If you are new to running, it is essential that the development of endurance starts slowly and progresses at a sensible level. Most coaches advocate an increase in distance run of no more than 10 per cent a week, otherwise there is a risk of injury. Clearly, athletes aiming for long distance events such as the 5,000 metres and 10,000m will need to place more emphasis on the development

of endurance than those in the shorter middle distance events.

Much of this work is done during the autumn and winter months of the close season, during which time you can gradually increase your weekly mileage in preparation for higher-intensity work as the season approaches. Unless a strong aerobic base has been established before you start more intensive training, it is likely that performances and recovery will be poor, and the risk of fatigue and injury will be significantly increased.

Benefits

Endurance training improves the ability of the lungs to extract oxygen from air that is breathed in and strengthens the heart so that blood containing oxygen can be pumped more efficiently around the body. Within the muscles, the number of blood vessels transporting oxygen will be increased, as will the number of mitochondria (the sites within the muscle cells where the generation of energy occurs). All of these factors combine to increase the body's ability to utilise oxygen for the creation of energy and consequently improve your performance and recovery.

Running is excellent for endurance, working the cardiovascular system and core leg muscles.

Interval training

Mixing faster bursts of high-intensity running, followed by a short recovery, is an alternative to continuous steady running. Known as interval training, this technique has been followed with great success by runners for many years.

What is Interval Training?

By understanding that faster running places a greater demand on the anaerobic energy system, scientists have been able to show that it is possible to develop this aspect of performance by incorporating relatively short, high-intensity efforts within a training session. This has become known as 'interval training', when faster bouts of running are separated by short recovery times.

Interval training provides the basis for much of the training undertaken by today's athletes. Sprinters, who need to develop basic speed and power, tend to focus on short, maximum-effort sprints separated by long recovery intervals to ensure that their leg speed is maximised.

In contrast, middle distance runners normally sustain longer bursts of near maximum effort, separated by shorter periods of recovery. They do this in the knowledge that they are repeatedly attaining speeds that they would be unable to sustain in a single one-off burst. In doing so, their bodies adapt to the fatigue-inducing lactic acid that is produced and as a consequence they gradually become capable of tolerating faster running speeds for longer.

Similarly, long distance runners use interval training as a means of conditioning their bodies for sustained periods of hard effort. Their running phases tend to be longer, but at a slower pace, than middle distance runners, but the interval between each phase is still insufficient to allow full recovery. During most sessions, the pace sustained during the effort will be faster than their race pace, but the duration will be less. However, sports scientists have shown that the cumulative effort of fast running and short recovery times

Seasonal training

Track training varies according to the time of the year. Sprinters use the winter months for strength and conditioning, while middle and long distance runners switch to road and cross country races to build endurance. The weeks of spring are used for intensive preparation before the season begins, and with a coach you can develop a racing schedule for the competitive season that results in peak fitness for key events. During the autumn, a number of weeks are set aside for rest and recovery, during which the volume and intensity of training can be significantly reduced.

has the potential to result in significant improvements in performance.

Fartlek Training

Although many athletes and coaches undertake interval training in a formalised way, with set times and distances for running and recovery, a less formal method is known as 'fartlek' training, a Swedish term that means 'speed play'. This is a simple way of combining high-intensity efforts into a 'normal' steady run. The athlete increases the pace and effort during the run, then slow down for a short period of time to recover, but still continue running. This adds both increased intensity and variety to a run, and can either be structured or you can simply decide when to run fast and when to recover.

Training with a Coach

Interval training has three main variables that can be changed to alter the nature of the session, namely the frequency, the intensity and the time (of the effort and the recovery). A good coach will vary these in a manner that makes the session specific to the demands of your event, while gradually adding progression by increasing the difficulty of subsequent sessions, thus ensuring that you continue to improve.

Understanding how to correctly design and implement an interval training session is crucial.

Sprint interval training

Sprinters have very different training needs to those of middle distance and endurance runners. Sprint training needs to focus on maximum speed movements, developing leg speed and power that is needed to maximise velocity across the track.

100m and 200m Training

For 100-metre and 200m athletes, an interval session that creates fatigue is unlikely to develop leg speed. Therefore interval training for sprinters must involve maximum pace efforts, followed by long periods of recovery. Unlike middle distance and endurance runners, the creation of fatigue and high levels of lactic acid is not recommended or necessary when training.

400m Training

The situation is slightly different for 400m runners, where speed endurance becomes a greater challenge. By the second half of the race, 400m runners experience rapid increases in lactic acid levels, compromising their ability to sustain their running speed. By replicating this fatigue in training, 400m runners can condition and adapt their bodies to the effects of sustained, high-speed running, and interval training is an ideal way of achieving this. When interval training, 400m runners tend to run near-maximum effort phases, separated by short periods of recovery.

One of the mistakes made by 200m runners moving up to 400m is a failure to undertake the speed endurance training that is necessary for the one-lap event, in the hope that their leg speed alone will be sufficient to produce winning times.

How the professionals train

In Great Britain, the majority of top international athletes will receive funding from the National Lottery via UK Sport, which allows them to train on a full-time basis and get access to properly qualified coaches, as well as sports science and sports medicine support. As a result, their training schedules are designed to suit their individual needs and monitored on a regular basis. They receive advice on crucial areas such as sports nutrition, to ensure that they are fuelling their bodies properly for both training and competition, as well as psychological and lifestyle support to ensure that they are properly prepared and focused for major events. Most elite athletes train twice a day, as well as undertaking regular flexibility sessions and receiving sports massage to aid recovery. Usually, elite athletes have one day a week scheduled for recovery, which may involve either complete rest or a light, low-intensity training session. Before the start of a season, the coach and elite athlete identify the priority events at which a peak performance is desired and the training schedule will be designed to reflect and achieve this objective.

It is sometimes suggested that 800m runners who have developed speed endurance may be better equipped than 200m runners to adapt to the 400m event. By being prepared to use interval training, 400m runners can induce the fatigue experienced during the latter part of the race, thus developing the speed endurance that is essential for sustained, high-speed running.

The distance you choose to run has a big impact on the training plan you undertake.

47

Diet

The human body is in many ways similar to a car – no matter how well it is capable of performing, if it is given the wrong fuel it will not function properly. In recent years, one of the reasons for advances in athletics performances has been improved sports nutrition.

Fat Busting

Whenever you eat, your energy comes from three main food groups – fat, carbohydrate and protein – which also contain vitamins and minerals that are essential for health and wellbeing. For hundreds of years after the Ancient Olympic Games, there was a belief that as human muscle consists largely of protein, an athlete's diet should also contain large amounts of protein to keep the muscles properly fuelled for exercise. However, during the 20th century, scientists were able to show that in fact it is the carbohydrate (or glycogen) in the muscles that provides the energy needed for both endurance and sprint events, not protein. Furthermore, while it contains plenty of energy, fat is an inefficient fuel that only makes a contribution to energy supply during low-intensity exercise. Even the leanest humans have ample stores of body fat, so there is no need to add additional fat to your diet.

Carbohydrate

The body's reserves of carbohydrate are stored as glycogen in muscle and the liver, which unfortunately only allows around two hours of moderate-intensity exercise. While this is not likely to be a problem for events other than the 20-kilometre and 50km Race Walks and the Marathon, it can pose a problem for athletes who are in regular intensive training, particularly if their daily diets are low in high-carbohydrate foods.

Sports nutritionists therefore recommend that athletes consume a diet that is consistently high in carbohydrate foods. Carbohydrate comes in two basic forms – starches such as bread, pasta, rice, cereals and potatoes, and sugars, such as jam, marmalade and

What to eat before and after training

Before – It is not advisable to eat closer than two to three hours before a training session, so that food in the stomach has time to digest. Your last meal should contain plenty of carbohydrate and consist of foods that are familiar and easily digestible. Foods that are high in fat and protein should be avoided since they take a long time to digest and provide little in the way of useful energy.

After – It is important to eat as soon as possible after training because this is the best time to replace the energy that your body has used and the best foods to eat are those containing plenty of carbohydrate.

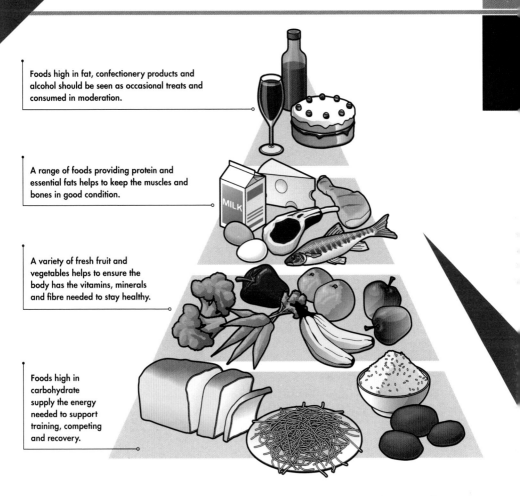

Foods high in fat, confectionery products and alcohol should be seen as occasional treats and consumed in moderation.

A range of foods providing protein and essential fats helps to keep the muscles and bones in good condition.

A variety of fresh fruit and vegetables helps to ensure the body has the vitamins, minerals and fibre needed to stay healthy.

Foods high in carbohydrate supply the energy needed to support training, competing and recovery.

MILK

honey. A sensible mix of both types of carbohydrate, with the main emphasis on starches, is the best possible way for you to replace the energy that you use when training and racing.

Protein

There is no evidence to suggest that eating large amounts of protein can increase muscle strength, although many athletes still consume high-protein diets in the hope that this will be the case. Providing you eat a variety of foods that contain plenty of carbohydrate as well as fresh fruits and vegetables, which are high in vitamins and minerals, it is likely that you will receive all the fuel that your body requires, as well as the vitamins and minerals that are needed to sustain a healthy function of the body.

Hydration

Runners lose fluid, mainly by sweating, regardless of the distance they run, and the climate they are running in. Replacing this fluid and combating dehydration is critical, since just a small loss of fluid can have disastrous effects on a runner's performance.

Fluid Loss

During exercise, the muscles produce heat and, unless this heat is lost, body temperature can quickly start to rise to potentially dangerous levels. To counteract this, one of the main ways the body loses heat is through sweating, whereby the evaporation of fluid from the surface of the skin causes body heat to be lost.

Scientists have measured sweat rates in excess of 3 litres per hour in athletes training or competing in hot conditions and the replacement of this lost fluid is essential if sweating is to continue and body temperature is to be controlled. As sweat is lost the body dehydrates, and research has shown that once sweating has caused a reduction of more than 2 per cent of body weight – something that can easily happen within the first hour of exercise – both physical and mental performance soon start to suffer.

Dehydration

It is vital that you begin a training session or competition properly hydrated, attempt

Sports drinks

Sports scientists have found that drinks containing a specific blend of carbohydrate and minerals (electrolytes) will optimise the rate at which fluid and energy are absorbed into the body, thus providing fuel and combating dehydration. These drinks are known as isotonic drinks – the concentration of particles is similar to that found in the body, hence they are absorbed very easily. Stronger drinks, containing higher concentrations of particles, are known as hypertonic drinks. These are absorbed less quickly, but can provide large amounts of energy. Drinks containing a lower concentration of particles are hypotonic – while these can be absorbed quite easily they have only a limited impact on the replacement of energy reserves and are best suited for fluid replacement only.

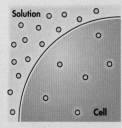

Fluids with a higher concentration than the cells take longer to be absorbed.

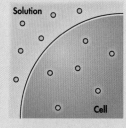

Fluids with the same concentration as the cells are absorbed rapidly.

to stay hydrated during the event and rehydrate effectively afterwards. While dehydration can affect any athlete, it is of greatest concern to endurance runners who have to sustain long and intensive periods of physical activity, especially when conditions are hot or humid. Not surprisingly, Marathon runners and walkers face the greatest challenge from dehydration, not only in their races, but also in training as well. Nevertheless, staying properly hydrated is vital for all athletes, including sprinters and middle distance runners, who will lose fluid whenever they train.

Fluid Replacement

By checking body weight before and after a training session, it is possible to estimate the amount of fluid that has been lost and which therefore needs to be replaced. Every kilogram of weight lost is equivalent to approximately 1 litre of fluid, which then needs to be consumed to fully rehydrate. Drinking alcohol and caffeine is not a useful means of rehydrating, since in large or strong quantities these can actually increase the rate at which the body dehydrates.

It is important to take fluids as dehydration can greatly affect athlete performance.

A simple self-help guide is to check your urine colour – if it is dark then it is likely that dehydration has occurred. Drinking small amounts of fluid frequently should help to replace fluid that is lost and keep the urine a lighter, straw colour.

Light coloured urine shows good hydration and dark urine indicates dehydration.

The mental edge

In any sport, the margins between success and failure are very small and athletics is no exception. Training programmes focus on the development of the body but unless your mental approach to training and competition is correct, the chances of success are greatly reduced.

Sports Pyschology

Today's elite athletes spend time working with sports psychologists to prepare themselves for competition, developing mental strategies that enable them to cope with different situations. In the heat of intensive competition retaining mental composure can make all the difference between winning and losing. While some athletes prefer to psyche themselves up before a race, others prefer to remain calm and introverted. It is therefore vital that you find a mental strategy that creates the best possible environment to suit your specific needs, prior to the start.

An inevitable physiological reaction before the start of a race is the body's release of the hormone adrenalin, which helps to prepare the body for action. However, too much adrenalin can cause anxiety and nervousness, and even feelings of nausea. Learning how to cope with this, and remain calm, is something that you will need to practise and rehearse.

Be Positive

Retaining a positive attitude throughout a race is essential for success, whether beating an opponent or achieving a personal best time. Many athletes will admit to having lost a race before even starting, simply because they were not

in the right frame of mind and gave themselves little chance of winning or doing well. Conversely, even if up against an opponent who may in theory have a faster time, it is still possible to increase the chances of success through self-belief and a positive approach to the race, which can in turn unsettle the opponent.

Self-belief and a positive approach are essential for success whether it is beating an opponent or achieving a personal best.

Adopting the right mental approach to training is also important. Few athletes find training easy and retaining the motivation to tackle hard sessions or to train on dark, wet nights is something that all athletes have to work at. A positive mental attitude to training is essential if the quantity and quality of training that is needed to succeed is to be completed and this is one of the reasons why training in a group or with a club can be of great benefit.

It is easy to have the right approach to training and competition when things are going well. A harder test of mental aptitude is when things go wrong or your performance is not as good as expected. When this inevitably happens, you will need to refocus and set new targets, while analysing the reasons behind the disappointment. It is important not to allow failures to create a negative approach – instead use them as a catalyst and motivation for future success.

Drugs in sport

In a sport where the difference between success and failure can be measured by a 100th of a second, the temptation to cheat can be strong. But those who use illegal performance enhancers do so at the risk to their own health.

Illegal Drug-Taking

The use of performance-enhancing drugs in athletics can be traced back to the start of the Modern Olympic era, when stimulants were believed to be essential in helping athletes cope with demanding endurance races. Unfortunately, the use of performance-enhancing drugs has extended in parallel with advances in medical research, and many products originally designed to treat medical conditions have since been adopted by athletes and less reputable medical support staff as a means of improving their performance.

Performance-enhancing drugs can cover a range of areas including: steroids, which help athletes to build muscle and recover more quickly; painkillers, which mask injury and discomfort from fatigue; stimulants, which can raise heart rate and alertness; and drugs used to treat medical conditions such as asthma or heart conditions. WADA publishes and regularly updates its list of banned substances, which, if found in an athlete's urine or blood sample, risk a long-term suspension from the sport.

Drug Testing

In the UK, athletes have to provide UK Anti-Doping with their whereabouts for one hour of each day. This is so that drug-testing officers can always locate them for a drug test, regardless of whether it is their competitive season. Repeated failure to declare whereabouts, or failure to be in the designated location at the designated time, can also lead to a suspension or ban from competition.

Since athletics was rocked by a drug-testing scandal in 1988 – Ben Johnson, the winner of the 100m in the Seoul Olympic Games, was stripped of his title and banned after testing positive for

Anti-doping agencies

The World Anti-Doping Agency (WADA) was established in 1999 to promote and coordinate the battle against the use of drugs in sport. In turn, many nations set up their own national Anti-Doping Agencies affiliated to WADA, responsible for the fight against drugs in sport in their own countries. The United Kingdom's agency is UK Anti-Doping (UKAD), funded by the Government, which works closely with all UK sports in the battle against drugs.

the anaerobic steroid stanozolol – the sport has been at the forefront of the fight against the use of performance-enhancing substances. It is a battle that the sport, and the anti-doping agencies, must continue to fight and win to protect not only the integrity of athletics, but also the young athletes who aspire to compete in a drug-free environment in future years to come.

Medical Conditions

WADA operate a system of strict liability for all athletes, which holds them accountable for all substances found within their bodies when tested, and thus responsible for all food, drink and medication that they take. Athletes with injuries or medical conditions will often benefit from remedial medicines. However, it is vital that they check what these contain and get clearance from their medical adviser first. A Therapeutic Use Exemption (TUE) can be issued by a medical officer, allowing an athlete to take certain drugs for a medical condition, normally for only a short period of time, even if it is on the WADA banned list.

Warming up

Preparing your body for exercise is essential and this process is normally referred to as warming up. Every training session or competition should begin with a warm-up.

Benefits

Warming up serves a number of important functions:

- It raises body temperature, which reduces the risk of injury and increases range of movement by making the muscles and surrounding tissues more pliable.
- It increases the flow of blood and oxygen to the muscles to help with energy production.
- It helps to mentally prepare you for exercise.

The timing and nature of the warm-up are crucial. Too soon before the start of training or a competition and you will not be properly prepared; too long, and you run the risk of losing the benefits before the training or race starts. The warm-up must be at an intensity that raises the body's temperature and prepares it for action, but not so intensive that it uses up valuable energy stores or increases lactic acid levels. The nature of the warm-up will also depend on the event and prevailing climate – a sprinter will undertake a very different warm-up procedure to a Marathon runner, and all athletes will need to warm up in a different manner on a cold, damp day compared to days when conditions are hot and sunny.

The Warm-up

The warm-up can be divided into three distinct phases. The first stage requires some gentle jogging and upper body movements, usually lasting for 5–10 minutes, and is designed to raise the heart rate, increase body temperature and stimulate blood flow to the muscles.

The second stage is a series of specific stretches focusing on many of the major muscle groups identified on pages 55–7, which will be used in the event to follow. This stage usually lasts for 10–15 minutes and it is vital

What to wear

At the start of the warm-up you should wear outer layers such as a tracksuit, particularly when conditions are cold. These can be discarded once you start to feel warm, since excessive sweating is not advisable during the warm-up period. If necessary, outer layers can be replaced once the warm-up has been completed in order to retain body warmth prior to the start of the training session or race.

that muscles are never over-stretched to the extent that they become painful. Stretches should take the muscle to the point where some tension is felt, held for a few seconds and then relaxed.

Once the second stage of the warm-up has been completed, you should spend a further 5–10 minutes performing some slightly more intensive running, including drills and faster strides. Ideally, there should be a gap of no more than a few minutes between the cessation of the warm-up and the start of training or a race.

Hamstring (standing)
Put your foot on a waist-high stationary object (a steeplechase hurdle, for example) and slowly lean forward, reaching down the shin until you feel a stretch in the hamstring.

Hamstrings (sitting)
Keeping one leg straight, bend the other so the foot rests against the knee. Slowly bend forward and using the hands, gently pull the upper trunk towards the knee of the straight leg, feeling a stretch in the lower back and hamstring.

Groin
Sitting on the floor with the soles of the feet together, and sitting up straight, the feet are grasped. The stretch is felt in both sides of the groin and down the inside of both thighs.

Hip flexors
Feet are placed a stride length apart with the front knee bent. The body weight is transferred forward, and the hips are pushed gently towards the floor. The stretch is felt at the front of the hip. Repeat other side.

Warming up

Incorrectly preparing can lead to injury or a poor performance, so knowing when and how to warm up before an event or training session is important for any athlete.

Lower back
Kneel down with your arms extended onto the floor. Gently push the head and upper body trunk towards the knees – you will feel this stretch in your lower back.

Gluteous maximus
Cross the foot over the upper thigh of the other leg and gently pull the knee towards the chest.

Waist
Keeping a vertical position, gently slide an arm down the outside leg, stretching the opposite side of the waist.

Shoulder and chest
Clasp the hands behind the back, keep the arms as straight as possible. Pull the shoulders back while breathing.

Calf
Lean against a wall with both palms against the object. The leg you want to stretch is back, several feet from the wall, your heel firmly positioned on the floor. Your other leg is flexed about halfway between your back leg and the wall. With your back straight, gradually lean forward until you feel the stretch in your calf.

Quadriceps
Hold a stationary object for balance with one hand and use the opposite hand to grasp the leg around the ankle, lifting it towards your bottom.

Triceps
The elbow is bent and grasped with the opposite hand. The hand is then gently pushed down the back. A stretch is felt in the back of the upper arm. Repeat other side.

Back and shoulders
Place your feet shoulder width apart and facing forward. With your fingers linked, the arms are pushed out straight with the palms to the front. The arms are then twisted and pushed to one side. The stretch is felt on the outside of the shoulder and in the centre of the back. Repeat other side.

Warming down

After exercise, whether training or a race, it is important to gradually return your body to normal, rather than stopping suddenly. This process is referred to as the warm-down period and is an important first stage in your body's recovery process.

Benefits

During hard exercise heart rate, body temperature, blood flow and lactic acid levels will have increased. By steadily jogging, walking and stretching for a period of around 10–15 minutes afterwards, it is possible to gradually reduce these physiological responses to values approaching normal. This will help you to recover more effectively, while also providing you with an opportunity for mental reflection and evaluation of the preceding race or training session. When conditions are cold, the warm-down is best conducted wearing outer layers such as a tracksuit or wet top.

Muscle Soreness

There is a theory that the pooling of lactic acid within the muscles after exercise causes muscle stiffness and soreness one to two days later, and that this can be avoided by warming down.

However, scientific evidence suggests that this is not the case, since lactic acid levels return to normal relatively quickly after exercise, even if there has not been an effective warm-down; it is more likely that post-exercise muscle soreness is as a result of micro-damage to muscle fibres that can cause some intra-muscular bleeding and swelling, which in turn leads to soreness. It is unlikely that the warm-down will prevent this, but it can still help to reduce stiffness in the joints and muscles.

The warm-down need not be as long or as complex as the warm-up.

Multi-event cooling down

In competitions where athletes are taking part in multiple events, with minimal recovery time between each of them, the cool-down can become part of a much longer process that enables an athlete to remain in a state of readiness before recommencing the warm-up for the next event. This is usually preferable to allowing the body to revert to a complete state of rest and then beginning the warm-up process from scratch for a second time.

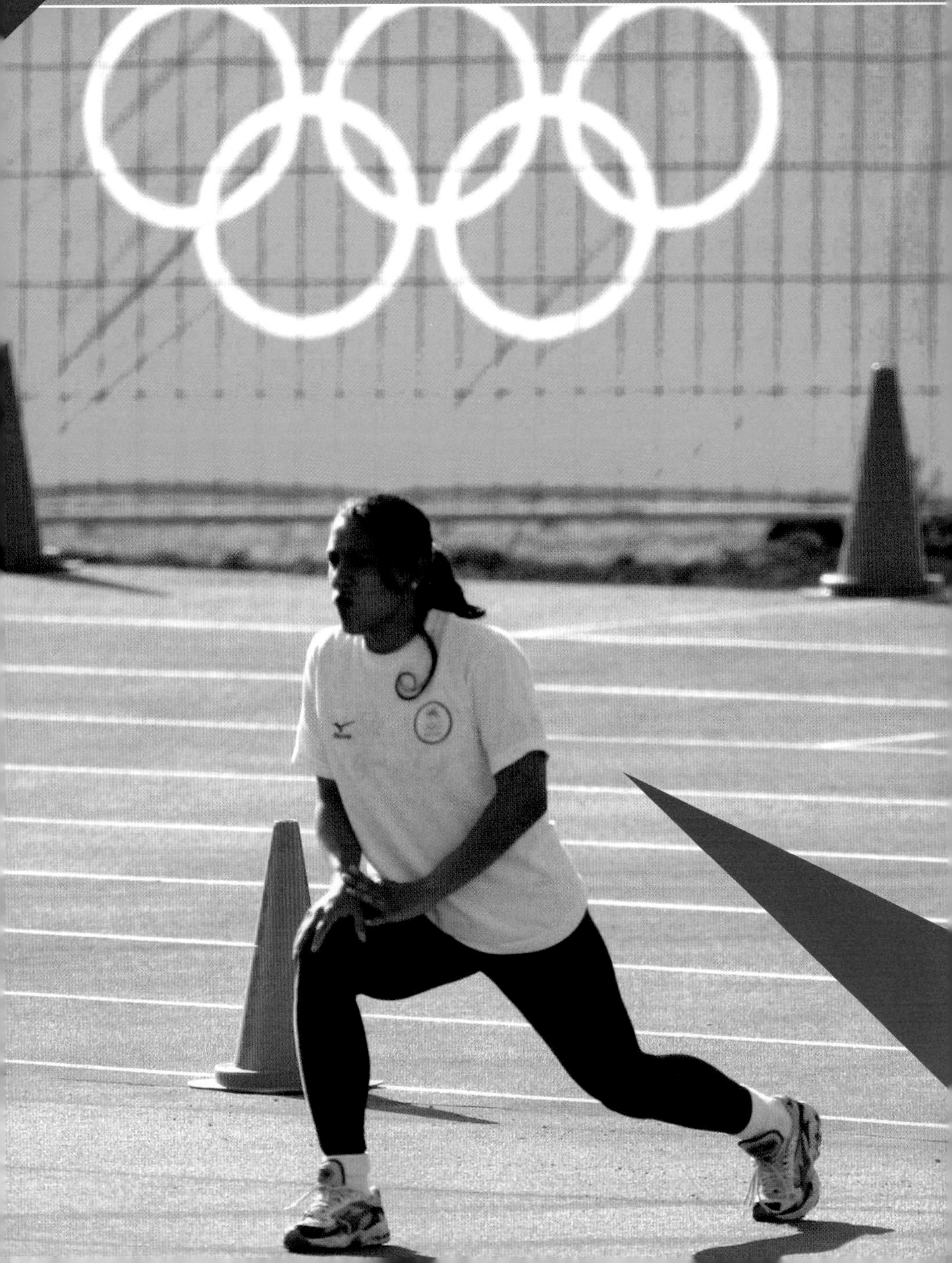

Weights and circuits

A properly designed and implemented weight and circuit training programme can be an important part of any athlete's training plan, but is of increased importance in the sprint and middle distance events where speed and power play a major part.

Weight training, as the term suggests, is based on the use of either rigid resistance machines or non-rigid free weights. Circuit training is a series of exercises that use the body's own weight as the resistance and are normally undertaken in sequence based on a set time or number of repetitions. Both have a part to play in your preparation, but must be part of an integrated training regimen – there are some who believe that weight and circuit training programmes are the essential and often dominant ingredient for success, yet this is rarely the case, and they should not replace running sessions.

Weight Training
There are a number of key guidelines that must be adhered to when weight training:

- Start slowly, using light weights and seek advice from an expert coach.
- Safety is paramount – learn the correct techniques and warm up properly.
- If using free weights, never work alone.
- If a running session is performed on the same day, this should be after, not before, weight training.
- Sessions should be between 30 minutes and 1 hour in length.
- During the off-season and preparation stages, two to three sessions a week are sufficient.

One of the main physiological benefits of weight training is an increase in the diameter (not the number) of muscle fibres, which in turn creates a larger, stronger and more powerful muscle. Additional muscle bulk is not advantageous for middle distance or endurance runners, who require extra energy to carry increased weight around the track, so weight training for these events should focus on developing strength endurance, using relatively low weights and resistances, and high repetitions (number of lifts). For sprinters, the extra muscle gained from weight training can lead to a reduction in joint flexibility, so it is vital that weight training is combined with a regular stretching and mobility programme.

Weights and circuit training can form an important part of an integrated training regime and the results will show in your track performances.

Circuit Training

Circuit training is a far simpler form of strength training than weight training, normally requiring only minimal apparatus. There are a variety of exercises and routines that can be adopted – the exercises are normally performed in a rotational sequence during which the number of repetitions of each exercise, and the number of rotations (or circuits) can be changed. Circuit training can be performed individually or in groups, with a coach controlling the time spent on each exercise and the number of circuits. It is always possible to add variety to a circuit training session and the format allows you to work within your own capabilities. A modern variation on circuit training is the outdoor 'trim trail', which enables you to work outside and combine a running session with a series of resistance exercises.

Injuries

Injuries are an occupational hazard of any sport. However, by understanding the main causes of injury, there are steps that you can take that will help to reduce the risk of an injury occurring.

Overuse Injuries

When running, the majority of injuries are caused by overuse, poor technique, inadequate recovery or ill-fitting clothing (particularly shoes). The level of training that results in an overuse injury will vary considerably from one athlete to another, and will depend on the volume and intensity of training and running that an individual does, as well as their background and experience. Trying to do too much too quickly is a common problem, especially in novice runners keen to improve their fitness and performance quickly. Most coaches and sports scientists recommend an increase in training volume of no more than 10 per cent a week, along with at least one day of rest each week that gives the body a chance to recover and adapt. Trying to increase training volume or intensity too quickly places an overload on the body that it cannot cope with and this will inevitably result in injury. One of the most common overuse injuries is a stress fracture, a hairline crack that usually appears in one of the bones of the lower leg, caused by the repetitive impact of feet hitting the ground.

Technique Injuries

Technique is often difficult to change, but many runners whose style looks uncomfortable may in fact be running in a manner that suits them, without excessive risk of injury. The angle at which the foot hits the ground can cause injury – in some runners the foot may turn outwards, known as overpronation, which causes stresses on the ankle and lower leg that can result in injury.

Injuries form an unfortunate part of an athlete's career but preparation and extra care can help minimise them.

Clothing and Footwear

Minor injuries such as abrasions and blisters are invariably the result of ill-fitting clothing or running shoes. Petroleum jelly can be used to help prevent chafing, particularly on long runs, and investing in appropriate running clothing, rather than leisure gear, is crucial. When buying running shoes, a good running shop should be able to advise on the best size and type of footwear to suit your style, weight and weekly mileage.

Recovery

Most injuries will recover with time. However, in cases where injuries are serious or persistent, it is advisable to seek the opinion of a doctor, who may make a referral to a specialist sports medicine physician or a professional such as a chartered physiotherapist. Once an injury has recovered, you should not return to training too quickly or expect to immediately resume at the pre-injury training intensity or volume, otherwise the risk of the injury reoccurring will be greatly increased.

Training troubleshooting

Judging when to train, and when not to train, can be both difficult and frustrating. Learning how to recognise the symptoms of illness and injury, and developing coping strategies to deal with them, are important for athletes at all levels.

Colds and Fever

One of the most frequent afflictions to affect many athletes is the common cold. This may be because scientists believe that immediately after a long run or intensive training session the body's immune system is temporarily suppressed, which can increase the chances of viral or bacterial infections. The general guideline if you are suffering from a cold is that training can continue, albeit with a slightly reduced volume and intensity, providing the symptoms are above the neck and consist of nothing more than a bunged nose or sinuses. However, if the symptoms are below the neck and include a sore throat, coughing or muscular aches and pains, then training needs to cease until the symptoms disappear.

Similarly, if the body temperature is elevated, and there is likelihood of influenza or a fever, training needs to be halted. Continuing to exercise when suffering from influenza or a fever can have very serious long-term consequences and greatly extend recovery time.

For any other illnesses it is important to seek medical advice from a doctor as quickly as possible. Be prepared to take the necessary time off to allow your body to recover properly before resuming training. When you start training again, it is important to recognise that some fitness will have been lost and initially some easier sessions are likely to be more tolerable and beneficial.

Staying Fit When Ill or Injured

With the exception of illnesses where complete rest is recommended, there are activities that you can undertake that will help to maintain fitness during an enforced lay-off. Depending on the nature of the problem, these could include cycling, rowing, swimming and the use of gymnasium machines such as cross trainers and steppers. The main benefit of these activities will be to maintain the fitness of the cardiovascular system, but inevitably some fitness in the peripheral areas, especially the legs, will be lost. Maintaining flexibility through regular stretching while injured is also important, and daily intake of calories needs to be reduced to reflect the decrease in energy expenditure.

Loss of fitness after around one week of inactivity is negligible, but if there has been two weeks of inactivity you should resume your training with a series of lighter sessions. Once a lay-off exceeds one month, there will be an evident loss of fitness; you should work with a coach to refocus your training programme, ensuring that when training resumes there is an initial reduction in volume and intensity, followed by a progressive increase in workload that is sensitive to your recovery.

Sprint technique drills

The 100 metres and 200 metres sprints can be divided into four distinct phases; the start, the acceleration phase, the peak velocity phase, and the finish. Getting these right is crucial, and sprinters must train specifically for each of them.

The human body has two types of muscle fibre – slow-twitch fibres, which are predominantly found in long distance runners, and fast-twitch fibres, of which there are a high proportion in sprinters. Scientists have shown that the proportion of these fibres is largely determined at birth, so sprinter training often focuses as much on developing technique as it does trying to improve basis speed.

Sprint Technique

At the start, sprinters have their weight evenly distributed through the arms and feet while in the crouch position. At the sound of the gun, they drive out of the crouch in a predominantly horizontal position, before gradually moving into a vertical position and the stage of transition into a normal running style. After this, they continue accelerating to maximum speed, which they then attempt to sustain for the rest of the race (see also pages 70–5).

Sprint Drills

Sprint drills can help to develop the appropriate technique for each stage of the sprint and some basic examples of these are illustrated below:

- Flicks – Distance 10 metres. Flick your heels to your bottom.
- Raised knees – Distance 10m. Raise your knees as high and as quickly as possible, taking short strides.
- Bounding – Distance 50m. Take long strides concentrating on driving with maximum effort with your rear leg, aiming for increased height and distance with each stride.
- Foreleg extension – Distance 20m. From a walk, raise your knee as high as possible, then extend your lower leg as far as possible as if clawing the ground.

In addition, providing a resistance to sprinting using either a hill, harness (held by a partner) or a tethered weight (such as a rubber tyre) can help to develop technique and power.

Sprinter training focuses as much on improving athlete technique as on speed.

Stay Relaxed

A key factor for successful sprinting is relaxation. If a sprinter becomes tense whilst running, their muscles tighten and their range of movement and speed decrease. Ironically, tension is often caused by trying too hard, and can therefore occur much more easily towards the end of a race or training session. As a result, sprint training must always take place when an athlete is fresh, and not fatigued, with coaches and athletes working together using techniques to help the athlete to stay relaxed.

A common relaxation technique is often known as an 'inertia run', where the athlete covers the first 30m at maximum speed from a 'sprint start' position, then uses momentum to stay as relaxed as possible over the next 50m, gradually slowing to a stop whilst remaining completely relaxed. Other techniques included 'acceleration – deceleration' runs, where athletes reach peak speed then relax to a tension free state in which running speed is maintained, before accelerating again when speed starts to drop. Since fatigue must be avoided the duration of this drill will depend on the conditioning of the athlete.

Track disciplines in detail

Track athletics offers the chance for individuals with varying physiques and abilities to compete over a range of distances. Whether lean, light endurance runners or muscular powerful sprinters, the challenge of reaching the finishing line at the front of the field is one that all athletes strive to achieve.

Sprint events — 100m, 200m and 400m

Sprinting combines excitement with strength, speed and graceful movements. The strong, powerful physiques of sprinters, combined with their rapid speed of movement across the track, means that the sprint events often provide the highlight of an athletics event for many spectators.

Physical Requirements

Whereas fatigue during the 100 metres is minimal, the 200m and 400m both result in athletes having to run at non-maximal speeds for some parts of the race. Since energy has to be obtained rapidly, sprinting uses the body's anaerobic energy system, which results in the build-up of a substance called lactic acid in the muscles and blood, rapidly causing fatigue.

Biomechanical analysis of the 100m and 200m events has found that, on average, men complete the 100m in 43–45 strides, compared to around 48–52 strides for women. To complete the 200m, men take between 83 and 85 strides, compared with between 92 and 105 strides for women.

Clothing and Footwear

A sprinter's clothing has to be light since excess weight requires more energy and reduces speed. However, due to the powerful forces produced by the muscles when sprinting, many athletes like to run in tight-fitting Lycra-type, which supports the muscles and retains warmth, thus reducing the risk of injury. Advances in clothing technology mean that manufacturers are always trying to develop clothing that gives extra aid to sprinters, either through physiological benefits, such as increases in blood flow to the muscles, or biomechanical benefits including decreased air resistance or increased muscle power.

Spikes are essential footwear for sprinters – the spikes are screwed into the sole of the shoe and the maximum length allowed is 9 millimetres.

However, usually much shorter lengths will be used, depending on the track surface and conditions. Sprinters only impact on the track with their forefoot, so spikes are only found on this part of the shoe and not in the heel. A sprinter's running shoes will need to be light, yet capable of withstanding the enormous forces that are produced during races.

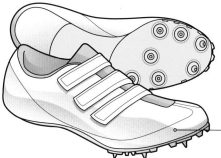

A sprinter's running spikes are light and strong, with seven short spikes on each foot providing grip.

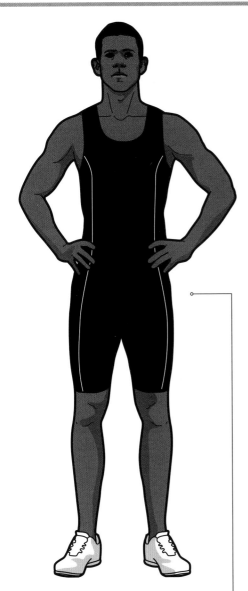

Advances in clothing technology have resulted in clothing that is designed to increase support and blood flow, and reduce injury.

Track Standards

UK Athletics, the national governing body for track athletics in the UK, have established National Standards for all track events, for both senior and junior athletes. These are shown in the Standards to Aspire to tables and are compared with the current Olympic record for each event.

The tables show the progression that an aspiring Olympic champion should be aiming for. If your times are significantly slower than the standard for your age, this should not stop you from joining a club, receiving coaching and enjoying track athletics. If you are close to the standards and show a good rate of progression, be aware that dedicating yourself to regular training is essential if you are to continue progressing to the highest levels.

Standards to Aspire to

100m

	Senior	U20	U17	U15	U13
Men	11.50	11.70	12.00	12.70	14.20
Women	13.20	13.30	13.50	13.70	14.80

200m

	Senior	U20	U17	U15	U13
Men	23.40	23.80	24.50	26.20	29.70
Women	24.10	24.90	25.30	26.00	31.50

400m

	Senior	U20	U17	U15	U13
Men	53.00	54.40	55.50	61.00	–
Women	64.0	65.00	–	–	–

100m and 200m techniques explained

Given the fast, rapid nature of the sprint events, understanding the rules and getting off to the best possible start are essential to give the best chance of success.

Race Rules

In elite races, a sprinter reacting to the starter's gun in less than 0.10 seconds will be disqualified.

In non-elite races where electronic starting is not used, false starts are at the discretion of the starter.

Athletes must remain within their designated lane at all times. Touching either line at the edge of the lane is considered to be outside of the lane.

The upper torso is the part of the body that needs to cross the finishing line to register a finish.

The Start

The first seven to eight strides of a sprint constitute the start phase, and these strides are generally considered the most important in the race. While less crucial in the 200 metres than the 100m, getting off to the perfect start has an impact on speed for the rest of the race, as well as having a psychological effect on other competitors.

Having adopted the start position, reacting quickly to the sound of the starter's gun is the first vital part of the start. Most runners can react within 0.16 to 0.24 seconds – at elite level where starts are monitored electronically, a reaction time faster than 0.10 seconds is not thought to be possible, so will lead to disqualification, whereas at club level, the starter will judge whether an athlete has moved before the sound of the gun.

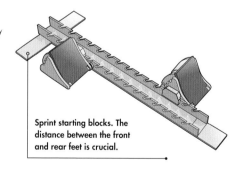

Sprint starting blocks. The distance between the front and rear feet is crucial.

'On your marks' – The sprinter begins by settling into their starting blocks.

'Get set' – The sprinter rises into a crouch position with their weight on the front foot and hands, looking down the track.

The use of starting blocks enables an athlete to focus as much force as possible in a horizontal direction at the start, and this phase has often been likened to a plane taking off, as the athlete drives forward from the blocks, slowly rising to a vertical position by the time the seventh or eighth stride has been reached. The emphasis is on driving forward with the legs and reducing the amount of rotational movement in the arms and upper body.

Technique Tip

- In the 200m, angle your starting blocks so that they point towards the apex of the bend – this reduces the distance that has to be covered and minimises the impact of the bend on the start phase.

Race conditions

Track surfaces will impact on sprint times – harder surfaces tend to produce faster times as they produce better propulsion than softer surfaces. Climate also has an effect – warm conditions are more conducive to rapid muscle contractions, so tend to produce faster times. The thinner air found at altitude improves sprint times, as does a following wind. However, in the 100m and 200m, if the following wind exceeds 2m per second, the time cannot be used for record purposes.

'Go' – Drive out of the blocks with the rear leg.

Accelerate rapidly, gradually rising to a vertical position and avoiding unnecessary swaying or sideways movements.

100m and 200m techniques explained

Learning how to accelerate and finish properly, and how to cope with the forces produced when running around a bend, are skills that sprinters must acquire.

Acceleration

Most sprinters continue to accelerate for the first 40 metres of a race. During this phase the force produced by the legs pushing off from the ground is crucial, generating forward and upward propulsion forces that are up to four times body weight.

Peak Velocity

For the remainder of the race, the athlete will try to maintain peak velocity – in top sprinters speeds of between 10m and 11m per second are achieved. Sprinters try to stay relaxed, minimising head movement, keeping the shoulders relaxed, while ensuring that they 'paw' rather than hit the ground with their leading legs to minimise any negative braking forces.

The Bend

Centrifugal forces caused by running around a bend at speed can disrupt the running style and speed of many sprinters, particularly those who are large and have a long stride. The tightness of the bend is greatest on the inside lane, so while it is possible for runners on the inside to see their opponents, many prefer the outer lanes where the curve is less.

The Finish

The finish occurs when the sprinter's torso passes the finish line. A faster time can be achieved by 'dipping' – simultaneously flexing the hips and

pulling the arms backward to force the trunk to the line. While this frequently makes the difference between winning and losing a close race, too great a dip can result in over-rotation, causing athletes to fall and risk injury.

Technique Tips

- To counteract the centrifugal force of the bend lean slightly into the curve of the bend, use your left arm less and make greater movements with your right arm.
- Do not try to reach peak speed while running the bend of a 200m – instead use the exit of the bend, onto the straight, as a 'slingshot' from which you can accelerate to the finish line.

'Dipping' at the line can improve your finishing position but overrotation can lead to loss of balance.

Usain Bolt

Born in Jamaica in 1986, Usain Bolt first came to prominence in 2002, winning the 200m in the World Junior Championships, but it is his performances since 2008 that have gained him global recognition. At the Beijing 2008 Olympic Games he won gold medals at 100m, 200m and in the 4x100m Relay, setting world records in all three. At the 2009 World Championships in Berlin, he repeated the feat, setting world records for the 100m of 9.58secs, and 19.19secs for the 200m. Taking into account his reaction time at the start, Bolt's average speed for the 100m is 23.7 miles per hour (38 kilometres per hour).

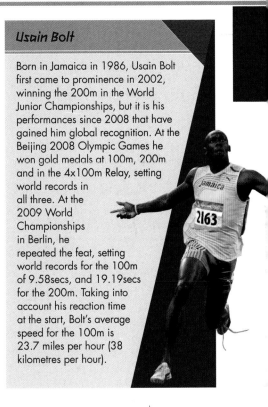

400m techniques and tactics

The 400 metres is often referred to as the hardest of all track events, involving not only basic speed, but also considerable speed endurance for the latter part of the race. No athlete is capable of running the entire distance flat out, so pace judgement is crucial.

Race Tactics

There is no single formula for success in this one-lap event. Athletes have achieved success and fast times by employing different tactics – some have started quickly and tried to minimise fatigue during the latter stages of the race, while others have found it best to start more slowly, then increase their speed over the last 200m.

Leg Speed vs Speed Endurance

400m runners generally tend to be either 200m runners with fast leg speed who can demonstrate good speed endurance or middle distance (particularly 800m) runners who have excellent speed endurance and reasonable leg speed. A great example of a sprinter who could demonstrate excellent speed endurance is the American athlete Michael Johnson, who won an Olympic gold in both the 200m and 400m, and holds world records in both events. In contrast, the Cuban athlete Alberto Juantorena was more suited to middle distance running, becoming the first man ever to win Olympic gold medals at both the 400m and 800m at the Montreal 1976 Games.

Basic Speed

As performance times have improved, so coaches and scientists have suggested that the importance of basic speed as a prerequisite for successful 400m is increasing. Since speed endurance is generally easier to train and improve than basic speed, there is therefore an increasing trend for top 400m runners to be sprinters who have trained to achieve good speed endurance, as opposed to middle distance runners who have tried to develop basic speed. To emphasise this, the current men's world 400m record, set by Michael Johnson in 1999, is 43.18secs, which equates to covering each 100m in 10.80secs, at an average speed of 20.7 miles per hour (33.3 kilometres per hour).

A variety of race tactics and sprint styles make the 400m one of the Olympic Games' most fascinating events.

Technique Tips

- Focus your training on achieving good basic speed and excellent speed endurance, as these are the two key characteristics of top 400m runners.
- Condition your body to cope with the high levels of lactic acid that will inevitably be encountered towards the latter stages of the race.

Personal best times

It has been suggested that the best 400m time you can achieve can be estimated by doubling your personal best 200m time and adding 3.50 seconds. Hence the estimated best 400m time for an athlete with a 200m personal best of 23.00secs would be 23 x 2 (+3.5) = 49.05secs.

100m, 200m and 400m training tips

Top sprinters are defined by their high percentage of fast-twitch muscle fibres. These are determined at birth, and contract quickly and powerfully to produce the forces needed to propel an athlete at high speed over the ground.

Sprint Speed

Your sprinting speed is simply the result of your stride rate multiplied by the stride length. Top sprinters combine both of these elements to produce fast times, but work with their coaches to break down the different components that influence stride rate and length so that they can be developed in training. While the genetic pre-determination of muscle fibre type will have a significant impact on your capacity to achieve the highest standards as a sprinter, there is no doubt that appropriate training can result in small but nevertheless significant improvements in performance.

Off-season Training

The planning of your annual training programme should be a high priority. The training year normally commences after the rest period that follows the competitive track season. This rest is essential so that you have time to recover both physically and mentally.

Unlike middle distance and endurance runners, who spend much of the autumn and winter months competing away from the track on roads and cross country, the majority of sprinters will use this period as a time for conditioning and preparation, with little, if any, competition. Some top athletes may compete in indoor competitions, but

Sprinters rarely compete off-season and use the time for conditioning and preparation.

Cathy Freeman

Cathy Freeman became the first Australian Aboriginal athlete to win gold at a major track championships when she won the 400m Commonwealth title in Auckland in 1990. She went on to win the world 400m title in 1997 and 1999, and came to global prominence when she became the first competing athlete to light the Olympic Flame, to mark the start of the Sydney 2000 Olympic Games. Under intense pressure, she won the Olympic 400m title in front of her home crowd in a time of 49.11secs, carrying both the Australian and Aboriginal flags on her lap of honour. She retired from athletics in 2003 to establish her own charitable foundation.

most will see this as part of their preparation for the outdoor season, rather than a key focal point in their racing year.

Work with a coach, if you have one, to analyse the successes and weaknesses of the previous competitive season and develop an off-season training programme that will build on these. During the early stages of the off-season, the majority of your training will move indoors to the gym, working to improve strength and power so that the foundations are in place for more intensive speed work.

Drills and Track Work

Gradual introduction of drills (see pages 66-7) and continual flexibility work will ensure that you can gradually increase the volume and intensity of training as the season approaches, eventually moving onto the track to work on the specific phases of your event. Progressing too quickly into track work, due to either inadequate recovery or a poor conditioning phase, can quickly and easily result in injury.

4x100m and 4x400m Relays

The relay events – 4x100 metres and 4x400m – involve teams of four athletes who aim to pass a 50-gram, 28–30-centimetre-long baton around the track as quickly as possible.

4x100m Race Rules

For the 4x100m Relay, the baton must be passed from one sprinter to another within a 20m changeover zone, which straddles each 100m section of the race. The changeover zone is marked on the track by yellow lines and is preceded by a 10 metres long pre-changeover zone (marked by an orange line) in which the outgoing runner can stand. The handover of the baton must occur within the changeover zone.

Baton Handover

The difference between a successful and unsuccessful sprint relay often rests with the efficiency of the baton changeovers. There are two techniques for passing the baton in the 4x100m Relay, namely the 'up pass' and the 'down pass'. The down pass is quicker, but can be a higher risk strategy,

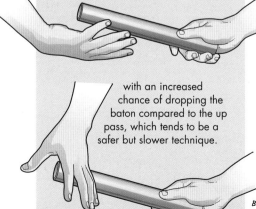

with an increased chance of dropping the baton compared to the up pass, which tends to be a safer but slower technique.

Technique

The first and third legs involve running a bend, so these legs should be completed by athletes who are particularly suited to bend running. To minimise the distance covered, the runners of the first and third legs keep to the left-hand side of their lanes, therefore meaning that the outgoing runners on legs 2 and 4 stand towards the outer, right-hand side of their lanes to avoid a collision. This is made easier if runners completing the first leg hold the baton in their right hands, thus allowing space for the second-leg runners to stand in the correct position and receive the baton in their left hands. Similarly, the third-leg runners stand to the left of their lanes, receive the baton in the right hand and hand it to the final-leg runner's left hand.

Check Marks

There is a responsibility on the outgoing runners to begin accelerating from the pre-changeover zone into the changeover zone at exactly the right time, ensuring that they are approaching maximum speed when the baton is received, but are still within the changeover zone. This is done with the help of 'check marks', which are normally placed on the track between 5m and 8m from the start of the pre-changeover zone. The outgoing runners start accelerating as soon as the incoming runners have reached the check marks and await a call from the incoming runners to signal the point at which they present a steady hand to receive the baton.

Relay Changeover Zones

Standards to Aspire to

4x100m Relay

	Senior	U20	U17	U15	U13
Men	46.00	46.80	48.00	50.80	–
Women	52.80	53.20	54.00	54.80	–

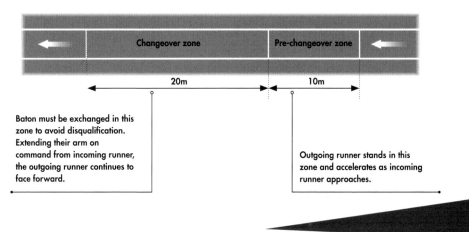

Changeover zone   Pre-changeover zone

20m   10m

Baton must be exchanged in this zone to avoid disqualification. Extending their arm on command from incoming runner, the outgoing runner continues to face forward.

Outgoing runner stands in this zone and accelerates as incoming runner approaches.

Relay Baton Changeovers

Right to left changeover

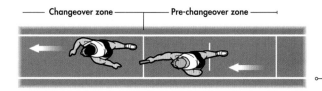

Changeover zone ———— Pre-changeover zone ————

First and third leg runners hold baton in their right hand and keep to inside of the bend.

Left to right changeover

Second and fourth leg runners hold the relay baton in their left hand. Incoming runner gives an audible signal for outgoing runner to extend receiving arm.

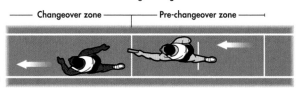

Changeover zone ———— Pre-changeover zone ————

4x400m Relay techniques and tactics

In major events such as the Olympic Games, it is traditional for the finals of the relay events to be held at the end of the competition, since they frequently create an exciting and highly competitive spectacle.

Lanes

In the 4x400 metres Relay, the first 500m is run in lanes, so the starts are staggered even more than in the individual 400m. While the first runners complete the entire 400m in lanes, the second runners only run the first 100m in lanes before moving to the inside of the track.

Changeover

The changeover is simpler than that of the 4x100m Relay. The outgoing runners stand on a line 10m from the finish line, and make visual contact with the incoming runner before starting to accelerate just before the incoming runners arrive.

On the third and fourth legs, the outgoing runners line up along the finish line in the order that the incoming runners are arriving, with the leading athlete's team on the inside of the track, moving outwards for the lower-placed teams. This can cause congestion and barging when races are close and positions are changing over the last few metres of the finishing straight.

Baton Handover

The incoming runners must remain on the left-hand side of the lane, thus passing the baton to the left hands of the outgoing runners, who must therefore switch the baton to their right hands at some point during their leg.

Technique tip

At handover, switch the baton from your left hand to the right at the start of your leg, prior to getting into your running rhythm.

Relay Tactics

There are varying tactics that teams can employ with their relay squad, although it is normal to assign the fastest squad members to the first and final legs.

It is vital that runners on the first three legs run at maximum pace, to ensure that they present the best possible opportunity for the final-leg runner to maximise the team's position.

Standards to Aspire to

4x400m Relay	Senior
Men	3:32
Women	4:10

The finale to the Games, its speed and the unknown element of the baton changeovers make the 4x400m a compelling spectacle.

100m, 110m and 400m Hurdles

The Hurdle events are run over three distinct distances: 100 metres and 110m for the women's and men's sprint hurdles respectively, and 400m. For all three distances, a total of ten barriers must be cleared, but the height of the barriers varies for men and women in each event.

Physical Requirements

Hurdlers need excellent flexibility to cope with the physical demands of clearing the hurdles, as well as producing the forces needed for take-off and to absorb those felt on landing. It is also an event where inclement conditions, such as strong winds or a wet track, can have a significant impact on technique and performance.

Hurdles

The hurdles are designed to fall over if hit but athletes can be disqualified if they knock over the hurdles intentionally. The 100m and 110m hurdles are higher than in the 400m event – 106.7 centimetres for men and 84cm for women. The first hurdle is 13.72m from the start line for men and thereafter every 9.14m. The first hurdle is 13m from the start for women and subsequently every 8.50m.

The 400m barriers are 91.40cm in height for the men and 76.20cm in height for the women. For both men and women, the distance between the hurdles is the same: the first is 45m from the start line and thereafter they are at 35m intervals.

The 400m Hurdle event was introduced into the Paris 1900 Olympic Games for men, but not until the Los Angeles 1984 Games for women. There is some suggestion that the height of the hurdles is too low for the women's event, which, it is claimed, favours 400m runners over athletes with good hurdling technique.

Ed Moses

A 400m hurdler, born in the USA in 1955, Moses is best remembered for his remarkable winning streak of 122 consecutive races, spanning nine years, nine months and nine days between 1977 and 1987. He also won Olympic gold medals in the 400m hurdles at the Montreal 1976 and Los Angeles 1984 Games, but was prevented from competing in the Moscow 1980 Olympic Games by the US boycott. He won the 400m world hurdle title in 1983 and 1987, and was the first athlete to regularly use a 12-stride pattern between the hurdles. He retired after winning bronze at the Seoul 1988 Games, and became a major reformer for drug testing in track and field.

Standards to Aspire to

110m Hurdles

	Senior	U20	U17	U15	U13
Men	18.00	18.50	–	–	–

100m Hurdles

	Senior	U20	U17	U15	U13
Women	18.00	18.60	–	–	–

400m Hurdles

	Senior	U20	U17	U15	U13
Men	63.00	64.00	65.00	–	–
Women	74.00	75.00	–	–	–

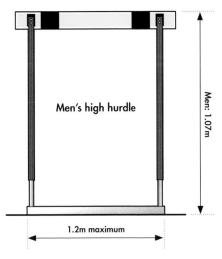

Men's high hurdle

Men: 1.07m

1.2m maximum

High hurdles

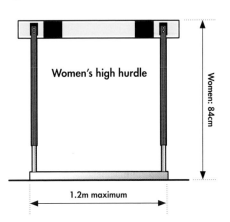

Women's high hurdle

Women: 84cm

1.2m maximum

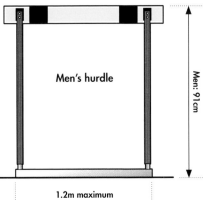

Men's hurdle

Men: 91cm

1.2m maximum

Hurdles

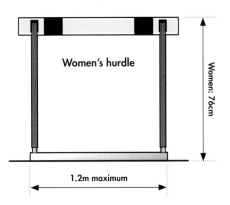

Women's hurdle

Women: 76cm

1.2m maximum

100m and 110m Hurdle techniques

These events combine the speed of a sprinter with the technique and agility that are an essential part of hurdling.

Race Rules

The rules for all Hurdle events are the same. Runners begin in starting blocks and athletes are only disqualified if a hurdle is knocked down intentionally.

Any athlete who allows either leg to drop below the horizontal plane of the hurdle while clearing it (thus allowing a leg to go around the outside of the hurdle) will be disqualified.

If athletes are forced to run outside of their lanes by other competitors, and gain no material advantage from doing so, they will not be disqualified. Furthermore, athletes who run outside of their lanes on the straight, or who cross the outer line of their lanes on the bend, will not be disqualified providing no other runner has been impeded.

Technique

While basic speed is essential, technique is equally important. The stride pattern from the start, and between each hurdle, is critical, and often a hurdler with good technique will be able to beat an opponent with better sprinting speed.

Lead and Take-off Legs

Most hurdlers have a preferred lead leg, which is extended first over the hurdle in a slightly bent position. The other leg

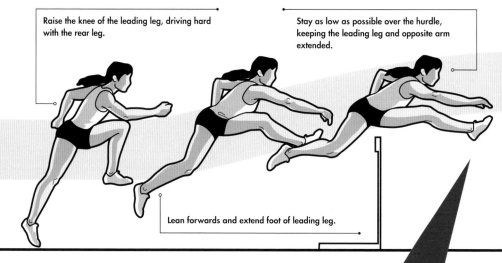

Raise the knee of the leading leg, driving hard with the rear leg.

Stay as low as possible over the hurdle, keeping the leading leg and opposite arm extended.

Lean forwards and extend foot of leading leg.

is the take-off leg, which is brought over the hurdle after the lead leg, and is often also referred to as the trail leg. The sprint start position (see page 74) may need to be adjusted to ensure that the take-off leg is in the correct position for the first hurdle, and athletes attempt to clear each hurdle with minimum vertical height and maximum horizontal velocity.

Take-off

Athletes normally take off approximately 2 metres from the hurdle, with the heel of the lead leg just clearing the barrier. The hips are flexed, bringing the trunk and upper body forward, so that the body's centre of gravity remains low. The knee leads the trail leg over the hurdle and is pulled over as quickly as possible.

(see page 74)

Technique tips

- If you can only manage four strides between hurdles you will need to alternate your lead and take-off legs or use a five-stride technique.
- Taller hurdlers with a long stride may find that three normal strides brings them too close to the next hurdle, so they will need to reduce their stride length to ensure optimal hurdling technique.

Clearance

On clearing the hurdle, the lead leg must snap down to the track, usually at a point approximately 1m in front of the hurdle, quickly followed by the trail leg so that stride length and momentum are maintained. To ensure optimum pace, athletes then take three further strides before the next hurdle, when the process is repeated.

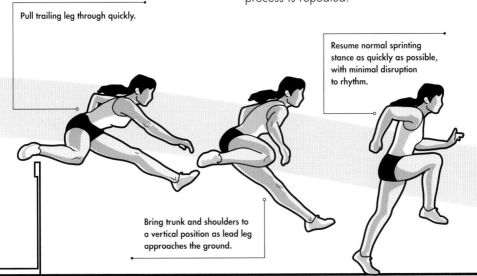

Pull trailing leg through quickly.

Resume normal sprinting stance as quickly as possible, with minimal disruption to rhythm.

Bring trunk and shoulders to a vertical position as lead leg approaches the ground.

400m Hurdle techniques explained

The 400m Hurdles is, not surprisingly, considered to be one of the hardest of all Track events, placing the highest demands on an athlete's speed, technique, speed endurance, strength and mobility. As with the 400m flat event, the 400m Hurdles is run entirely in lanes.

Technique

The hurdling technique is similar to that used in the 100m and 110m Hurdle events – athletes use a lead leg to gain initial clearance over the barrier, followed by their trail leg. However, the lower hurdle height normally means less forward lean of the trunk than in the other Hurdle events.

Stride Pattern

Correct stride pattern between the hurdles is essential for success in this event, which combines with fatigue and technique to determine the number of strides required to complete the 35m distance between each hurdle. The hurdler establishes a rhythm from the start to the first hurdle and the number of strides is predetermined to ensure that the correct leg is used for take-off. This is usually between 20 and 24 strides.

Thereafter hurdlers select a stride pattern that suits their ability – selecting an odd number of strides between hurdles (for example 13, 15, 17 or 19 strides) ensures that an athlete is able to take off and lead with the same leg at each hurdle. Selecting an even stride pattern may be quicker for some hurdlers, but requires an ability to take off and lead with alternate legs.

Technique tips

- If you are able to lead with your left leg you will be at an advantage because you can adopt a running position that is more closely aligned with the curve of the track. To be able to lead with your left leg over the first hurdle adjust accordingly your starting blocks and stride pattern over the first 45m.
- Try to develop the ability to take off and lead with either leg as this makes the transition in stride pattern far easier and more efficient during the latter stages of the race.
- If you are a beginner, you may require a second change in stride pattern between the eighth, ninth or tenth barriers.

Increasing the Number of Strides

After the fifth or sixth barrier, lactic acid levels start to build up in the muscle and blood, resulting in increasing fatigue. As a result, most hurdlers are unable to sustain their initial stride pattern and are consequently forced to switch to an increased number of strides between hurdles. The efficiency of this transition is crucial to success in the event. To continue taking off and leading with the same legs, most athletes will add an additional two strides to their pattern between hurdles, for example switching from 13 to 15 or 15 to 17 strides. However, athletes who are capable

of taking off and leading with either leg may only add a single stride to their pattern and this is a technique favoured by more experienced athletes.

Final Stages

Sensible distribution of effort throughout the race is crucial, since starting too quickly can quickly accelerate fatigue and have serious consequences for performance during the latter stages of the race. Upon clearing the final, tenth hurdle, athletes have a 40m sprint to the finish line.

Speed, endurance and technique are all necessary to become an accomplished 400m Hurdle athlete.

Middle distance — 800m and 1,500m

The 800 metres and 1,500m races are normally classified as middle distance events, involving a combination of both aerobic and anaerobic metabolism to complete the distances.

Olympic History

The 800m has always been an Olympic event for men, and although introduced into the Amsterdam 1928 Olympic Games for women, it was then suspended until the Rome 1960 Games due to the exhaustion caused to competitors. The 1,500m is seen by many to be one of the most prestigious of all track and Olympic events. It has been an Olympic event since the start of the modern era, but the women's event was not introduced until the Munich 1972 Olympic Games.

The Races

At non-elite level, the 800m starts from an arc at the finish line, but in elite races athletes have a staggered start and run the first lane in bends until reaching a green line on the track. Starting blocks are not used. Athletes in the 1,500m start from an arc at the beginning of the back straight and cover a total of three and three-quarter laps of the track.

In the 1,500m, and in 800m events where lanes are not used, there are often more than eight runners in a race, and as a consequence the early stages of the race often involve a significant amount of pushing and barging as athletes scramble for positions towards the inside of the track. As a result, it is quite common for runners to get tripped and fall in middle distance races, which are known to be the most physical of all track events.

Sebastian Coe

Born in London in 1955, Sebastian Coe become one of Britain's greatest ever middle distance runners, winning the Olympic 1,500m title and gaining silver medals in the 800m, at both the Moscow 1980 and Los Angeles 1984 Olympic Games. Coached by his father Peter, and a graduate of Loughborough University, Coe had a unique rivalry with fellow Britain Steve Ovett, which captured the attention of the media.

In 1979, Coe set three middle distance world records in 41 days, and in 1981 he set a world record time for the 800m of 1min 41.73secs, which stood until 1997.

Having retired in 1990, Coe led the victorious bid that brought the 2012 Olympic Games to London.

Lightweight clothing
provides support
while maximising
heat loss.

Lightweight running
spikes with cushioning in
the heel to avoid injury.

Start Position

An athlete usually starts in a semi-crouched position, with the torso and upper body leaning forward over the leading leg, which is slightly bent and with the toe behind the start line.

Standards to Aspire to

800m

	Senior	U20	U17	U15	U13
Men	2:04	2:06	2:10	2:22	2:38
Women	2:27	2:29	2:32	2:35	2:45

1,500m

	Senior	U20	U17	U15	U13
Men	4:20	4:25	4:35	4:35	5:25
Women	5:05	5:07	5:15	5:25	5:50

800m and 1,500m tactics

Middle distance athletes need to have good speed and the endurance to sustain this speed for two laps of the track. During a relatively short but fast race, there is little room for tactical error or mistakes, and athletes must learn how to cope with different tactics and strategies to be successful.

800m

In recent years, the 800 metres has become more akin to a sustained sprint event. As men's elite times approach 1min 40secs, athletes are required to produce two successive laps that are close to 50secs each. Ideally, an even pace around both laps is best suited to energy production and the avoidance of extreme levels of lactic acid.

However, in reality this is rarely possible. Some athletes who lack the basic speed required for a sprint finish will prefer to start quickly and run a fast first lap in the hope that it blunts the speed of faster finishers. Conversely, those who are known to have good speed that can be used in a sprint finish will prefer to keep the early pace slow so that they are in a position to 'kick' during the last quarter of the race.

In non-championship races, pace makers are often used to set a speed that gives the best chance of even lap splits and a fast finishing time. In most races, there is unlikely to be more than a 5secs differential between the first and second laps of an 800m race.

1,500m

The 1,500m is recognised as the most mentally and tactically demanding of the middle distance events. Attempting to set an even pace is equally important in the 1,500m, which places slightly more aerobic demands on the body than the 800m. The men's Olympic record time of 3:32.1secs, set by Ngeny of Kenya at the Sydney 2000 Olympic Games, is equivalent to 56.6secs for each 400m lap.

As with the 800m, there is a similar need for athletes to avoid being boxed in, although the slightly slower pace of

Front Runner

Due to the relatively short, fast nature of these races, the athlete at the front of the field has a major role to play in dictating the nature and pace of the event. This can often be advantageous to other runners in the field, who are able to focus on staying relaxed and tracking the leader, before finishing strongly. As a consequence, many coaches advise athletes not to take the lead unless they are fully committed to making a strong push to the finish line in an effort to win the race.

The 800m and 1,500m events are some of the Olympic Games most eagerly anticipated.

the race, and the longer distance, can make it easier for athletes to extricate themselves from problems should they arise. However, the additional laps and bends do mean that the distance implication of running in the outer lanes is much greater than in the 800m.

Athletes who set off too quickly in a 1,500m are almost certainly likely to experience a large spike in their lactic acid levels and, as the pace of the race is likely to remain fast, they are unlikely to have chance to slow to provide an opportunity for the levels to fall.

Athletes are often seen at near maximum pace for the first 100m of a 1,500m race in an attempt to be near the front at the end of the first (back) straight, and hence able to occupy the inside lane around the first bend. Other athletes will adopt a more cautious approach, conserving energy during the early stages and prepared to sacrifice some distance by occupying an outer lane for the first bend.

800m and 1,500m race challenges

Developing the right combination of speed, endurance and strength is a challenge faced by all middle distance runners. But understanding and avoiding difficult race situations is a critical component of success.

Getting Boxed In

Although there is an understandable desire to run towards the inside of the track in order to cover the shortest possible distance, middle distance runners who do so run the risk of being boxed in, a situation that occurs when the kerb on their inside, and surrounding runners beside and in front of them, prevent them from accelerating and overtaking other runners. This can seriously inhibit an athlete's chances of doing well in a race, particularly if it allows faster, unimpeded runners to accelerate away from the front of the field.

Some middle distance runners will elect to run a slightly longer distance in an outer lane rather than run the risk of getting boxed in, while others will hold back from the leading group of runners in order to get a clearer route, in the hope that they can close any possible gap with the leaders at the end of the race.

Race Etiquette

Many coaches and athletes would argue that there is no etiquette during middle distance races, which are accepted as being the most physical of all track events. Runners strive to be as close to the inside of the bend as possible to cover the shortest distance, yet also want to ensure that they are not boxed in, so

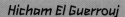

Hicham El Guerrouj

Moroccan athlete Hicham El Guerrouj was born in 1974 and won the 1,500m World Championship title in 1997, 1999, 2001 and 2003, as well as becoming a double-Olympic gold medallist by winning the 1,500m and 5,000m titles at the Athens 2004 Olympic Games, becoming the first man in over 80 years to win both events at the same Games. He was unbeaten in mile and 1,500m events in 2002, and became the first man to win IAAF Athlete of the Year titles in successive years in 2001 and 2002. After the Athens 2004 Games, El Guerrouj did not compete again internationally and retired in 2006.

as a result physical bumping, pushing and barging are normal and athletes are frequently tripped.

In races where no athlete is keen to run quickly at the front of the field, the pace can be slow, resulting in bunching of runners, which further increases the physicality of the race.

Athletes unwilling to partake in the more physical aspect of middle distance running may

wish to run in the outer lanes or towards the back of the field, but consequently run the risk of covering greater distances or being left behind should there be a fast break from the front of the race.

The middle distance events are regarded as the most physical of the track events.

800m and 1,500m training tips

Middle distance athletes need to combine aerobic training with anaerobic training, while also developing endurance and flexibility. Runners taking part in the 1,500 metres will put slightly more emphasis on aerobic training than 800m runners, while 800m runners will focus more on their speed.

Interval Training

Your training should involve a mixture of steady running, to develop aerobic fitness, and interval training (including fartlek running) to develop speed and speed endurance. You need to adapt your body to the utilisation of high volumes of oxygen by developing your cardiovascular fitness and oxygen uptake capacity. You also need to train your body to tolerate high levels of lactic acid and to be capable of 'buffering' or removing the lactic acid as it is produced.

Interval and fartlek training (see page 42–3) must be used in a manner that frequently replicates race pace and conditions you to sustain your race pace for extended periods of time. Recovery periods between the running phases of interval training must be short, and consequently many of your training sessions will need to be tough and require strong mental resilience.

Speed Work

Speed work is vital, and while you don't need to practise technique to the same extent as sprinters, you will need to work on the development of leg speed and running action. Much of the speed work should incorporate some degree of fatigue, since this replicates the demands experienced towards the end of a race.

Core Conditioning

Development of core conditioning and strength is also crucial, the latter being an area that is often neglected by middle distance runners. Circuit training is ideal as it enables you to develop strength and strength endurance without gaining large amounts of muscle bulk. Developing arm and upper body strength is not essential, but good abdominal and trunk muscles help to maintain posture and provide some resistance to the physical nature of many middle distance races.

Off-season Training

During the autumn and winter months, many middle distance runners switch from the track, to the road and cross country races. This is important, since it develops the aerobic endurance and strength that are essential foundations for a spring and summer track season. During the off-season, increase the total number of miles run each week and reduce the volume of high-intensity speed and speed endurance work. As the start of the season approaches, so the weekly mileage should gradually be reduced, while high-intensity training, including interval training and fartlek running, should gradually be increased.

Middle distance events require a unique mix of speed and endurance and their training reflects this.

3,000m Steeplechase

Part middle distance and part endurance, the Steeplechase is an event that places unique technical and physical demands on its competitors. The barriers are unforgiving, easily tripping athletes whose hurdling ability has let them down, something that is all too easy as fatigue increases.

Olympic History

Steeplechasing first appeared in the Paris 1900 Olympic Games, when men ran a distance of 2,500 metres. The distance varied, until 3,000m was adopted consistently from the Antwerp 1920 Games until the present day. Women had to wait a further 88 years, when the women's 3,000m steeplechase was introduced at the Beijing 2008 Games.

Physical Requirements

Steeplechasers must possess all the characteristics of middle distance and long distance runners, including endurance, speed endurance and speed. However, they must also have the flexibility and technique of hurdlers, as well as the strength needed to clear the barriers at high speed and absorb the impact forces of landing.

Barriers

The barriers are 91.4 centimetres high for men and 76.2cm high for women. Unlike the hurdles used in the 100m, 110m and 400m hurdle events, steeplechase barriers are not designed to fall over if hit, but will allow runners to jump on and off them safely. The water jump consists of a barrier with a pit of water 3.66m long immediately after the barrier, which is at a depth of 70cm immediately under the barrier, then sloping upward towards the track surface.

Anders Gärderud

Swedish athlete Anders Gärderud competed in the Olympic Games in the 800m, 1,500m and 5,000m before achieving success in the 3,000m steeplechase at the 1976 Montreal Olympic Games. Born in 1946, Gärderud was eliminated in the heats of the 800m and 1,500m at the 1968 Mexico Olympic Games, and had a similar experience in the 3,000m Steeplechase and 5,000m at the 1972 Munich Olympic Games, where he was beset by illness. However during 1975 he broke the world 3,000m Steeplechase record on two occasions, before winning the Olympic title in a dramatic finish in 1976, breaking his own world record in doing so with a time of 8:08.02. On retiring from the sport, Gärderud competed internationally as an orienteer, and now works as a coach and TV commentator.

Standards to Aspire to

3,000m Steeplechase

	Senior	U20	U17	U15	U13
Men	11:00	12:00	–	–	–
Women	14:00	15:00	–	–	–

The Race

The 3,000m Steeplechase takes place over seven full laps, plus a proportion of an eighth lap. The exact length of the eighth lap, plus the nature of the preceding seven laps, depends on the position of the water jump, which may be on either the outside or inside of the second bend. In total, athletes have to clear 35 barriers, of which there are 28 standard barriers and seven water jumps.

To ensure that the race always ends at the start/finish line, the start of the race moves depending on the position of the water jump. When the water jump is on the inside of the track, the start is

Shoes with an outer mesh enables water to flow out after the water jump.

midway down the back straight, but it is moved towards the home straight if the water jump is on the outside. This first barrier is 200m from the start and the first water jump is always on the first full (not partial) lap.

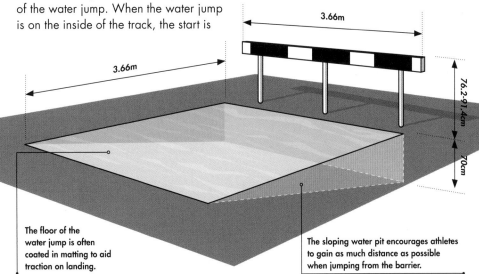

3.66m

3.66m

76.2-91.4cm

70cm

The floor of the water jump is often coated in matting to aid traction on landing.

The sloping water pit encourages athletes to gain as much distance as possible when jumping from the barrier.

3,000m Steeplechase techniques

Steeplechasers are challenged by the need to develop endurance, speed, speed endurance, strength, flexibility and hurdling technique in their training, which arguably makes this one of the hardest of all track events.

Technique

Many steeplechasers will try to establish a stride pattern between barriers to ensure an efficient hurdling technique, but this can easily be disrupted by other runners in the field and the long gap between the barriers. As a consequence, most top steeplechasers are able to hurdle barriers using either leg as their lead leg. Maintenance of a good hurdling technique is essential, especially when fatigued, since hitting a barrier almost certainly results in the athlete falling. While it is possible to step onto the top of each barrier and push off to continue, this is a much slower technique that results in the athlete losing considerable time.

The technique for the water jump, though, is different, with athletes invariably using the top of the barrier as a support from which to push themselves as far as possible out over the water, ensuring that they land in the furthest and shallowest part of the pit, and hence are quickly in a position to regain their running speed.

Tactics

Fields are often large in Steeplechase events and as a result there is considerable congestion as athletes approach the barriers, especially in the early part of a race. Some athletes prefer a cautious approach in the early stages, positioning themselves so that they have the time and opportunity to see the barriers clearly and adjust their stride pattern accordingly. Others will prefer to start more quickly, placing themselves towards the front of the field so that they can see and hurdle the barriers effectively.

During the race, the tactics are often similar to those in both middle distance and endurance running, with bumping and barging common. Conservation of energy is crucial, particularly during the early stages, since as fatigue increases, so technique decreases, which can be very detrimental to hurdling ability and an athlete's performance.

Training

During the autumn and winter months, athletes focus on their endurance and strength, with cross country and road running

On account of its large field of participants, the Steeplechase can become congested around the barriers.

an essential part of their programmes. In addition, weight and circuit training should be undertaken regularly and include exercises that develop core stability and the strength of the trunk and lower back, as well as the legs.

As the spring approaches, athletes decrease their weekly mileage and increase the intensity of their training by including more fartlek and interval training in their programmes. Strength work should still be continued, alongside regular mobility exercises, which should focus on the hips, hamstrings and groin.

Routine practice of hurdling technique is also important, and as the season approaches more speed work can be introduced to develop the basic pace and speed endurance that are essential for success in this event.

5,000m and 10,000m

Competing in endurance races on a track places unique physical and mental demands on athletes, and understanding how to develop and deal with the races' demands is an integral part of an athlete's training regime.

Physical Requirements

Both races place heavy demands on the athletes' aerobic system, requiring high levels of endurance and a well-developed oxygen uptake capacity. As well as their high aerobic requirement, both the 5,000m and 10,000m also require speed endurance and speed if they are to be run successfully. The 25 consecutive laps of the 10,000m also need considerable focus and mental endurance, with athletes often claiming that the repetitive nature of the laps makes a 10,000m race on the track much harder than 10-kilometre road races.

The current men's 5,000m world record of 12mins 37.35secs, set by Ethiopian Kenenisa Bekele, is equivalent to an average time of 60.6secs per lap, a pace that would have brought victory in the 1,500m at every Olympic Games until 1952! Bekele also holds the current 10,000m world record with a time of 26:17.53, equivalent to 25 consecutive laps of 63.1secs. In the women's events,

Bekele's Ethiopian compatriot Tirunesh Dibaba (see box) owes much of her success over both the 5,000m and 10,000m distances to her blistering pace over the latter stages of races.

Footwear

Whereas sprinters and middle distance runners tend to land each stride on their toes, endurance runners normally land on their heels. As a result, the running spikes worn by 5,000m and 10,000m athletes often have cushioning in the heel to reduce impact forces, and the length of the metal spikes will tend to be shorter since the need for grip at high speed is less.

The Races

The 5,000m and 10,000m are the longest distances run entirely on the track. The 5,000m consists of twelve and a half laps, starting from an arc midway at the beginning of the second bend. The 10,000m consists of 25 laps, using an arc at the start/finish line as the starting point.

Standards to Aspire to

5,000m

	Senior	U20	U17	U15	U13
Men	16:45	17:00	–	–	–
Women	20:00	20:30	–	–	–

10,000m

	Senior	U20	U17	U15	U13
Men	36:00	–	–	–	–
Women	42:00	–	–	–	–

The repetitive nature of the 5,000m and 10,000m races make them the most mentally demanding.

Tirunesh Dibaba

At the Beijing 2008 Olympic Games, Ethiopian athlete Tirunesh Dibaba won gold medals in both the women's 5,000m and 10,000m events, having already become the first female athlete to win both events at the 2005 World Championships. One of the reasons for her success is her incredible finishing speed – in the final of the 5,000m in Beijing, she completed the last kilometre in 2mins 36secs, the fastest ever kilometre split by any woman in a race longer than 3,000m. When winning the 2005 10,000m world title, her final lap was timed at 58.3secs. Dibaba has won a total of five world cross country titles, as well as the 10,000m title at the 2007 World Championships and the 5,000m title at the 2003 World Championships.

5,000m and 10,000m tactics

The sight of lean, fast endurance athletes intensely focused on coping with the demands of repetitive laps of a track is common in major track championships. Few other events create the same images of pain and fatigue, or place such heavy demands on mental focus and determination.

Race Start

Due to the length of the races, the start and early laps are not as critical as they are in the middle distance events. However, since lanes are never used, the fields are often large and bumping, and tripping can be a problem, so athletes still tend to cover the first few hundred metres quite quickly to gain the best possible position at the start of the race. Athletes always attempt to position themselves as close to the inside kerb as possible, since significant additional distance will be covered if a large proportion of the 12.5 or 25 laps is completed in one of the outer lanes.

Pace

It is very rare to find championship races where a constant pace is held throughout either the 5,000m or 10,000m distances. There are invariably periods during races where individuals, or small groups of athletes, will attempt to dictate the pace from the front, frequently injecting faster laps into the middle stages of a race in the hope that they will break away from others in the field. This is often the case when there are athletes in a race who are known to be fast finishers – their competitors will increase the speed during the middle laps in the hope that a build-up of lactic acid will decrease the pace of faster finishers. Such injections of pace may also create a small breakaway group of runners at the front of the field, which can then lead to a psychological advantage over the rest of the field, as the slower athletes find it hard to motivate themselves to produce the pace needed to close the gap.

Race Finish

Towards the end of a close race, the timing of the final increase in pace to the finish line is all important. Some athletes prefer to gradually increase their speed over the last few laps, forcing opponents into a sustained increase in pace. Others prefer a much shorter sprint to the finish, which may not occur until the final lap.

Team tactics

In major competitions such as the World Championships and Olympic Games, it is not unknown for runners from the same nation to run together as a team, taking it in turns to increase the pace, to the detriment of opponents, and controlling the lap times as a group. This is not illegal, as long as unfair tactics are not used on opponents.

Training

Much of the training for the 5,000m and 10,000m is endurance-based. Athletes run large weekly distances, often approaching 100 miles (160km), and include interval training and fartlek running to develop speed and speed endurance. During the winter they take part in road and cross country races, and the time outside of the track season is used to develop a sound aerobic base through training and racing.

At the end of the track season, most athletes will take a period of time to rest, before starting to increase their mileage to build up their endurance. Mobility training to develop flexibility is important, while the miles covered can be augmented with circuit training to develop the strength endurance that is needed,

particularly in the legs. The twists, hills and uneven, muddy ground of cross country are ideal for the development of leg strength during the off-season.

During the late winter and early spring, when the track season approaches, athletes start to decrease the distances covered in training and increase the intensity of their training with more interval and fartlek work.

Due to the distances covered in training, maintaining a high-carbohydrate diet is essential, as is adherence to a proper hydration strategy. The threat of dehydration, especially in hot or humid conditions, has resulted in the introduction of drink stations at most major events and championships.

The race pace often fluctuates in long distance events as a result of athletes' individual tactics.

The Marathon

There is nothing more inspiring than the start of a Marathon, whether featuring a small elite championship field, or the mass start of a big city event. Facing up to, and conquering, the demands of running 26.2 miles is one of the greatest challenges in sport.

Olympic History

Within major championships, the majority of the Marathon is completed on roads, with the start and finish normally in the main arena. The history of the event is well documented: the Marathon was held at the first Olympic Games of the modern era in Athens in 1896, when the distance was 40 kilometres. In the London 1908 Olympic Games this was increased to the present 26 miles 385 yards so that it could start at the Royal Palace of Windsor and finish in the Olympic Stadium at White City. The Marathon was first introduced into the Olympic Games for women at the Los Angeles 1984 Olympic Games – a race won by American athlete Joan Benoit in a time of 2hrs 24mins 52secs.

Physical Requirements

The 26.2 miles (42 km) of the Marathon makes it the longest of all the track events, placing extreme endurance demands on competitors. Runners have to take approximately 40,000 strides to complete the distance, resulting in high repetitive forces on the legs and lower body. A high and continuous demand for oxygen to provide energy taxes the cardiovascular system, and runners must have extreme levels of mental resilience to cope with the sustained effort that is needed to complete the race successfully.

Paula Radcliffe

In 2003, British athlete Paula Radcliffe became the fastest female Marathon runner of all time, setting a world record of 2:15:25 in the London Marathon, a time which no woman has come within 3mins of. Radcliffe won the World Half Marathon Championships in 2000, 2001 and 2003, and the World Cross Country Championships in 2001 and 2002. Despite becoming Marathon world champion in Helsinki in 2005, Olympic success still eludes Radcliffe, who failed to finish at the Athens 2004 Games and, suffering from the results of injury, finished 23rd at Beijing 2008. She has won the London and New York Marathons on three occasions each, and the Chicago Marathon once. Radcliffe has stated her intention to have one final attempt at the Olympic Marathon title at the London 2012 Olympic Games.

Standards to Aspire to

Marathon

	Senior	U20	U17	U15	U13
Men	3:00	–	–	–	–
Women	3:45	–	–	–	–

While all competitors must focus on the development of their aerobic system, good speed endurance is also important, particularly at the highest level. The winner of the Beijing 2008 Olympic Games men's Marathon title, Kenyan Sam Wanjiru, posted a time of 2:06:32, equivalent to an average speed of 4mins 49secs per mile!

With its unique history, the Marathon remains the Olympic Games' most iconic event.

Big City Marathons

Over the last 30 years, the Marathon has moved from an event that was almost exclusively run by elite, lean endurance athletes, to one that has become a popular challenge for the many thousands who take part in major city Marathons each year. For the vast majority of these runners, the challenge is to complete the Marathon distance, not to compete at it, yet the distance is such that it provides a challenge to runners of all abilities.

The majority of big city Marathons are held in the spring and autumn, avoiding the heat of the summer months. However major track championships are held in the summer and it is therefore common for championship Marathons to start early in the morning to reduce the effect of heat on the runners.

Marathon techniques and training

There is no easy way to train for a Marathon, and talent alone is never a substitute for hard work and sacrifice. Marathon runners have to be dedicated and willing to spend many hours on their own, running long distances, to develop the endurance that is fundamental.

Energy Stores and Race Pace

The Marathon is a race where correct pacing is essential. Marathon runners rely on the carbohydrate that they eat to provide them with muscle glycogen, which is their main source of fuel. Unfortunately, simply eating a high-carbohydrate diet won't allow the body to store all of the glycogen that it needs to complete the 26.2-mile (42km) distance, so Marathon runners complement their energy from glycogen with less efficient energy from their fat stores.

They do this by running slowly during the early stages of the race to ensure that they have enough muscle glycogen to get them to the finish line. If runners set off too quickly, the relatively inefficient metabolism of fat means that it is unable to provide the energy athletes need, so they burn their limited carbohydrate stores right from the start. Consequently, by the time the 18–20-mile (29–32km) distance is reached, all of the body's glycogen reserves have been used up and fatigue sets in very quickly. This is often referred to as 'hitting the wall', and is common when Marathon runners have failed to judge their pace correctly and covered the early miles too quickly.

Running more slowly in the early stages enables energy to be obtained from a combination of both carbohydrate and fat, and gives the runner a much better chance of running efficiently to the finish.

Training

Training for a Marathon is inevitably based on the development of endurance, and there is no substitute for a steady build-up in weekly mileage to gain the aerobic fitness that is essential for completion of the distance. Depending on running background, beginners need to start their

Your first Marathon

If you are competing in a Marathon for the first time, it is vital that you start with a realistic target time in mind, based on your performances and times set over shorter distances in your pre-race preparation. Convert this target time into a sensible pacing strategy that gives you a close-to-even pace for the entire race distance. This often feels very easy during the early part of the race, so do not make the mistake of setting off too quickly, as you will invariably pay the price later on.

training five to six months before the race, gradually increasing their weekly mileage and the length of the 'long run'. This 'long run' is a vital component of a training regime, and as the term suggests is the longest run of the week, usually performed at the weekend. It is also advisable to include some competitive

The Marathon athlete must manage their pace so they have enough energy to finish.

races during the build-up to a Marathon, such as a Half Marathon or longer events over distances between 16 and 20 miles (28 and 32km)

Elite Marathon runners use the winter months to build up their endurance, with a combination of high weekly mileages that include faster high-intensity sessions to develop speed endurance. They often train on two occasions a day, frequently resulting in a total running distance of over 100 miles (160km) per week.

Race Walking

Race Walking has a style and technique that sets it apart from all other events in track athletics. Requiring high levels of endurance, it also places sometimes controversial technique restrictions on athletes that can, and frequently do, lead to disqualification.

Olympic History

Race Walking was first introduced into the London 1908 Olympic Games and appeared over varying distances until the Melbourne 1956 Games, when both of the present Olympic distances of 20 kilometres and 50km were included for men for the first time. Women competed over a 10km distance for the first time at the Barcelona 1992 Games, with the distance increased to 20km at Sydney 2000. Women do not currently compete over the 50km distance at the Olympic Games.

As with the Marathon, in major events such as the World Championships and Olympic Games, the 20km and 50km races are held largely on roads rather than on the track, although the finish may be within the stadium.

Taking Part

Due to the lower impact forces associated with Race Walking compared with running, it is a sport that appeals to people of all ages. While there are a small number of specialist Race Walking clubs, most walkers belong to general athletics clubs that have a specific Race Walking section.

Races are over distances from 1 mile to 100 miles (1.6–160km), with occasional events over even greater distances. Since it can be difficult for novices to learn the technique of

Robert Korzeniowski

Korzeniowski is recognised as one of the greatest race walkers of all time. Born in Poland in 1968, he has won four gold medals at the Olympic Games and three World Championships. In the Sydney 2000 Olympic Games, Korzeniowski became the first ever person to claim both the 20km and 50km titles and in doing so successfully defended the 50km title that he had previously won at the Atlanta 1996 Games. He retained his 50km title for the third successive time by winning the gold medal at the Athens 2004 Games. As well as successes at the Olympic Games, Korzeniowski also won gold in the 50km walk at the World Championships in 1997, 2001 and 2003. He retired in 2004 to pursue a career in the media.

Standards to Aspire to

20km Race Walk

	Senior	U20	U17	U15	U13
Men	2:00	–	–	–	–
Women	2:30	–	–	–	–

50km Race Walk

	Senior	U20	U17	U15	U13
Men	6:10	–	–	–	–
Women	–		–	–	–

straightening the lead leg on contact with the ground, in the UK there are beginners' events where this rule is not applied.

Globally, and in the UK, the sport of Race Walking is increasing in popularity; events are held for Under 13s and many race walkers are able to compete into their seventies and beyond.

Race Walking events can be competed over events in excess of 100 miles (160km).

How to start Race Walking

The national governing body for Race Walking in the UK is the Race Walking Association (RWA), racewalkingassociation.btinternet.co.uk. The RWA organises championships and events for junior and senior athletes, and works with the English Schools Athletics Association and UK Athletics to develop talented walkers. Through their website, the RWA offer a free introductory pack to the sport, which provides information on how to get started, and contact details for local clubs and events.

The UK's National Race Walking Centre is at Leeds Metropolitan University leedsmet. ac.uk/sport, where top race walkers and coaches benefit from training sessions, first-class facilities and training camps.

Race Walking techniques and training

The principles of training are the same for race walkers and runners, although developing stride rate is crucial in Race Walking. Some aspiring walkers may be put off by their apparent ungainly image, but this is simply a reflection of the skill and endurance that a walker must develop.

Race Walking is much faster than regular walking and differs from all other track events since correct technique is essential for successful performance. The Olympic events of 20 kilometres and 50km are both extreme tests of endurance and as such the training reflects that of all other endurance athletes.

Race Rules

There are two key technique-based rules that race walkers must adhere to.

- The first is that the walker must always be in contact with the ground, which means that the toe of the rear leg must not have lifted from the ground before the heel of the front foot has landed.
- Secondly, walkers must ensure that their leading leg remains straight (not bent at the knee) from the point when the foot hits the ground, until the leg has advanced under the body beyond, the point where it is vertical.
- During races, judges will be positioned on the course to ensure that the rules are adhered to. If a judge deems that a rule has been broken a red card is issued, which is positioned on a board that is visible to walkers so that they are aware that an offence has been committed. If walkers are issued with three red cards during a race, they are disqualified. However,

the red cards must be issued by three separate judges, since no single judge may issue more than one red card to the same walker during a race. In international competitions, the red cards must also be issued by judges from different countries to avoid accusations of national bias.

Stride Rate

A combination of aerobic work and speed endurance training are essential components of a race walker's training programme. You will need to work on specific drills to develop stride rate (cadence), since race walkers' stride length is significantly shorter than that of runners due to the technical restrictions of the events. Pace is increased most effectively, and legally, by increasing cadence, not overstriding, and a rate of around 200 strides per minute is not uncommon among top race walkers. Similar rates are observed in 400m runners, while top Marathon runners will have a cadence of around 150 strides per minute, figures that emphasise the importance of rapid stride rate for walkers.

Correct technique is critical and closely monitored by judges during a race to prevent infringements.

Flexibility

You will need to spend considerable time working on the development of your flexibility, particularly the muscles of the legs, and your hips. This helps to make correct technique easier to achieve and sustain, while reducing the risk of injury.

The big day

Race day is the chance to reap the rewards from the hard work of training and compete against other athletes and personal targets. Getting race day right will make all the hard work seem worthwhile, but getting it wrong will lead to disappointment and frustration.

Race day

Any runner not feeling apprehensive before an important race is unlikely to perform well. There is nowhere to hide on an athletics track, so failing to perform well is hard to disguise. But even in coming last, an athlete can still perform well, by achieving a target or personal best.

Correct preparation for a race is critical to success, something that holds true for both experienced athletes and novices competing for the first time.

Pre-race Preparation

Preparation should start in the days before a race, with a decrease in training volume and intensity so that you are not fatigued. The day before a race should be one of rest, with at most very light jogging and stretching. During the days before a race, you should ensure that there is plenty of carbohydrate in your diet and that you remain properly hydrated. Alcohol should be avoided on the day before a race. While this preparation is important for athletes of all distances, it is particularly true of endurance runners whose performances will be impaired if their carbohydrate stores are not optimised.

Sleep Tight

A good night's sleep is important before a race, but you may find that your sleep suffers due to nerves. This is not uncommon, and while not ideal, a disturbed night of sleep is unlikely to have a major impact on performance.

Kit Checklist

Drawing up a checklist of kit that will be needed on race day is often advisable, since it is all too easy to leave something critical behind. As well as the basics such as running spikes, shorts, vest and tracksuit, other essential items such as snacks, a sports drink, safety pins and petroleum jelly are easily overlooked, so

Pre-race routine

- Draw up a checklist and pack your kit bag in good time.
- Avoid alcohol on the night before a race and try to get a good night's sleep.
- Find out the start time of your race and work backwards – wake up in time to have a carbohydrate-based breakfast and arrive at the start with time to spare.
- Stay properly hydrated before the race and have a light lunch if the race is in the afternoon.
- Begin your warm-up routine in good time and structure it so that you move seamlessly from the end of the warm-up to the start of the race.

Afterwards

- Preparation for the next race starts as soon as the last race has finished. You can ensure that your recovery starts properly by following some simple guidelines during the first few hours after crossing the finishing line.
- Cool down sensibly with some light jogging and stretching, but stay warm with extra layers of clothing if necessary.
- Have an isotonic drink to start replacing the fuel and fluid that have been used while racing.
- As soon as practical, eat a carbohydrate snack such as a banana or energy bar to give additional energy.
- Think back over the race – consider what went well and what went wrong, and focus on tactical lessons that can be learnt or aspects of fitness that might need improving.

are best packed the night before rather than on the day of the race.

On the Day

The location and time of the race are critical to the planning of race day. If a race is in the morning, and requires travelling, it is vital that time is allowed to wake up, eat breakfast, and arrive in good time. If the race is in the afternoon, breakfast is still important, but a snack or light meal should be consumed later in the day, but no closer than two to three hours before the race to give the food time to be properly digested. Meals and snacks should have a high carbohydrate content and high-protein or fat products should be avoided.

Nerves

Pre-race nerves affect competitors at all levels, but are often worse for novice athletes. They are related to the body's release of the hormone adrenalin, which has a role in preparing the body for

action. With experience, nervousness can be reduced through mental relaxation techniques, but can also help you to focus on the challenge of the race ahead. Beginning your warm-up routine will help to reduce pre-race nerves, and once a race starts, the physical and mental demands of the event normally result in nervousness completely disappearing.

Few experiences can match the excitement of a competitive race no matter what your level.

Competitive athletics in the UK

The governance of track athletics in the UK provides a structure for development of talent at all levels. From participation to podium, the sport is structured to provide the best possible to support and help to athletes, coaches, volunteers and officials.

The national governing body for track athletics in the UK is UK Athletics, (UKA), which oversees the development of the sport at grassroots level, as well as the selection and performance of elite athletes in major international competitions. In partnership with the home countries athletics associations, UKA works closely with over 1,400 clubs, as well as schools and local authorities, to develop and promote the sport. This includes the education of coaches and the certification of facilities, ensuring that a high-quality infrastructure is available to support athletes of all abilities.

The home countries athletics federations are affiliated to UK Athletics, with responsibility for the strategic development of the sport within their own country. They are:

England Athletics
englandathletics.org

Athletics Northern Ireland
niathletics.org

Scottish Athletics Ltd
www.scottishathletics.org.uk

Welsh Athletics
welshathletics.org

Each home country also has its own Schools Athletics Association, responsible for the development and administration of the sport in secondary schools. Award Schemes based on performance in each event are offered and promoted though schools and their physical education departments. In England, school children compete as Juniors (13 years of age but under 15 on 31 August of their current school year), Intermediates (15 years but under 17 on 31 August of their current school year), or Seniors (17 years but under 19 on 31 August of their current school year).

One of the key challenges facing developing athletes, and the sport, is management of the transitional period from school athletics to club athletics. Unfortunately, many athletes find it difficult to cope with the increase in standard faced when they stop competing as a Senior at school, and move into the 'open age group' club environment. Careful nurturing and exposure to appropriate competition is crucial for talented athletes during this phase, and the selection of the right club is therefore vital.

To assist with this, UK Athletics provide a 'Club Search' facility on their website to help athletes or parents find a club that is local to their home, and which suits their needs. Before joining a club, prospective athletes should enquire about training nights and training facilities (including whether the club has its own track), coaching opportunities (including the number and qualifications of coaches), opportunities for competition during the track and off-season, the size of the membership, and whether there are junior, senior and veterans sections at the club. Speaking with existing club members is advisable, and if possible request a trial visit to the club to join in with training, before deciding whether or not to join.

With over 1,400 clubs as well as schools and local authorities, the UK presents many opportunities for budding track stars.

Other challenges

Athletics is a sport that offers something for everyone, whether old or young, athlete or non-athlete. While running is an activity that can be continued well into old age, athletics offers other opportunities in areas such as coaching, volunteering and officiating that can be rewarding.

Masters Athletics

As a runner gets older, it is inevitable that physiological changes will result in an inability to achieve the performances of their youth. However age is not a barrier to participation in track athletics, since older athletes are able to compete in age-group-related events, run under the auspices of the British Masters Athletics Federation (BMAF, www.bvaf.org.uk).

The Federation currently has over 7,000 active athletes in the UK, including many who are over 70 years of age. The BMAF runs track and field, cross country and indoor championships, with competitions divided into five year age groups, giving older athletes the chance to compete against others of a similar age. Older runners competing in road running outside the track season will also find that they are able to compete as 'veterans', with their results judged against others in their age group.

Officiating

Officiating is both an essential and rewarding part of track athletics. Qualifications and training for officials is offered at four different levels. The first two levels are delivered by the appropriate home country federation, while the Level 3 and Level 4 awards are delivered by UK Athletics. Anyone

wishing to become an official can specialise in a range of areas, including timekeeping, starting, track refereeing and photo finish analysis. At the highest level, officials who make themselves available and who are good enough may be able to join the International Officials Group, and officiate in overseas competitions and championships.

Coaching

UK Athletics offers a modern and comprehensive career development pathway for coaches. Entry-level leadership awards are available for those interested in working with athletes in the early stage of their development pathway. The first step on the coaching ladder is a Coaching Assistant Award, followed by the Athletics Coach Award, completed over three days, and offering an opportunity for coaches to specialise in different areas, such as endurance or sprinting. Full details of the UKA Coach Education programme are available on the UK Athletics website.

Volunteering

Every athletics club relies heavily on volunteers to keep it operating effectively. Volunteers are at the heart of the sport, and volunteering requires little or no training – simply an enthusiasm for the sport and a desire to help out. The best way to volunteer is to visit a local club and offer to help – many of the roles are rewarding and challenging, such as Team Manager, Club Treasurer or Press Officer. Further information on volunteering opportunities and how to find a local club is available at the UK Athletics web site.

Masters events, coaching, officiating and volunteering can be just as rewarding as competing.

Further information

Finding out more about track athletics, and the coaching, training and science that underpin human performance, will increase your understanding, interest and success in the sport.

The popularity of track athletics, and running, has resulted in a wealth of information on all aspects of the sport, including training, nutrition, coaching, injuries and sports science. Whilst much of this is of real value and helps to increase understanding and raise performance levels, some of it is less reliable and should be treated with caution. Hence using reliable sources of information, particularly websites, helps to ensure that the information gained is helpful, safe and reliable.

Nutrition and training are particular areas where there is a great deal of misinformation – if a claim, product or training programme sounds too good to be true, then it probably isn't true, so treat it with extreme caution! Many athletes have wasted large sums of money on products claiming to provide a short cut to improved fitness and performance, but in reality these rarely work, and can sometimes be detrimental to an athlete's health.

The following is a list of reputable websites where more information on track athletics, training, nutrition and sports science can be obtained:

United Kingdom Athletics
uka.org.uk
The website for the governing body running the sport in the UK, with information on coaching, fixtures and local clubs.

England Athletics
englandathletics.org
The body responsible for the sport in England, with a website providing information on coaching courses, teams and the structure of the sport.

Scottish Athletics
www.scottishathletics.org.uk
A website providing information, news and statistics for athletics in Scotland.

Welsh Athletics
welshathletics.org
The official site of Welsh Athletics, with information on clubs, schools, fixtures, events and coaching.

Northern Ireland Athletics
niathletics.org
Specific information on the sport in Northern Ireland, with latest results, fixtures and details of clubs.

International Association of Athletics Federations (IAAF)
iaaf.org
The official website for the world governing body of athletics with global news, rankings, rules, results and statistics.

England Schools Athletics Association
esaa.net
The ESAA promote enjoyment of athletics in schools. They offer a range of award schemes and advice on a variety of topics, and produce regularly updated standards to help talented athletes achieve their potential in the sport.

Race Walking
www.racewalkingassociation.btinternet.co.uk
The official site for the governing body of race walking provides information on the sport and its history, how to get started, rules, and a list of local clubs and events.

Sportshall
sportshall.org
Sportshall provides an opportunity for children to compete and train indoors during the winter months. The website provides information on the Sportshall programme and the activities and opportunities that are offered.

Sportscoach UK
sportscoachuk.org
A body working with sports to recruit, develop and retain coaches, providing a range of courses and workshops to help the development of coaches at all levels.

UK Anti Doping
ukad.org.uk
The national body responsible for the management and implementation of anti-doping policy in the UK, with educational resources and the latest updates in the anti-doping science and medicine.

UK Sport
uksport.gov.uk
UK Sport invests in the development of systems to improve coaching, talent identification and performance in the UK. It also supports research programmes that will help to deliver elite performances at major championships and international events.

Index

Picture credits

The publishers would like to thank the following sources for their kind permission to reproduce the pictures in this book.